YOUR MIND CAN DRIVE YOU CRAZY

by
James A. Takacs

Delphi Books
Delphi Information Sciences Corporation
Santa Monica, CA 90401

ISBN-0-930306-34-1

Printed in the United States of America

Library of Congress Catalog Card Number 79-87577

To Chuck and Ann
with love...
Jim

Acknowledgments

This book exists because of the endless encouragement and goodwill I have received over the years from a group of people who have afforded me the opportunity to grow and to share. They challenged me, directly or indirectly, to challenge my own material (sometimes rather uncomfortably) so that I might separate the fanciful from the workable. I wish to acknowledge:

Paula, for being my friend, not just my mother.

Chuck and Ann Fina, my oldest and dearest friends, for their outspoken honesty.

Leonard Orr, for so ably demonstrating what it means to let people, all people, be who they are without judgment or interference.

Betsy, for allowing me to experience the extent of my poverty training.

Stephen Johnson, for nurturing me through a particularly harrowing slice of my life.

Patti, Barbara, Thelma, Carol, Mary, Louise, Barbara and Jennifer for demonstrating so effectively how power-

Acknowledgments

ful women really are.

The staff of Psychonetix for years of support, love, encouragement and good-humor and the staff of Everywomen's Village.

Stewart Emery for translating the truth into very clear and precise language.

The many, many people who have taken my seminars, listened to my words, tested my material and insisted I do my best.

And last but not least, certainly my acknowledgment of Reverend Ike, for being the powerful, joyful and alive individual that he is.

Thank you all!

Jim Takacs
Tarzana, California
January 1979

Contents

Introduction

Judy began over-eating the day Andy walked out on her. From her petite 112 pounds, she zoomed to a waddling 220. When she died the doctors mentioned something about cholesterol and heart strain, but all her friends knew Andy was responsible. That's crazy!

Charles hired a new secretary. She took shorthand at 110 words, typed at over 90, but also happened to look like Farrah Fawcett-Majors. Although Charles was a faithful and loving husband, his wife's smouldering jealousy grew so intense she became an alcoholic. Then of course, Charles paid attention to her. That's crazy!

Frank did his work well and pinned his hopes for the future on an upcoming promotion in Public Relations. Frank was a rather loud, outspoken individual so his boss selected somebody else for the job. Frank became so bitter and sullen, he was eventually fired. He moved around a lot in short-term jobs and his friends lost track of him. The last time they heard, he was a part-time night watchman at a fishing dock somewhere in San Pedro. Somebody said he was on drugs or something. The whole thing was crazy!

Mary had dreams of becoming a singer, but her marriage seemed to demand all her time. Under her pleasant exterior boiled anger and resentment toward her husband and it eventually controlled her behavior. The pleasant life in suburbia turned into a living hell for both partners in the marriage, hence the divorce. Her friends shook their heads sadly. It was crazy!

This is the kind of "crazy" aberrant behavior our minds inflict upon us in the daily conduct of our lives. It is the kind of craziness which takes our lives through obesity, heart attacks, lung cancer and a host of other physical conditions.

The human mind not only has the power to drive us crazy, it can literally kill us!

A book which proves beyond doubt that the mind can drive you crazy is no more valuable than a pamphlet which proves earthquakes cause damage. What you will learn by reading this book are the powers we all possess which not only keep the mind from exercising its destructive tendencies, but actually harness the mind's power for our own purposes of joy and freedom.

To proceed through life without exercising control over such a high speed and powerful energy source as the human mind, is like speeding down a busy freeway with your arms folded. The nature of an automobile is such that the power and speed of the vehicle has an inherent ability to kill you, so you learn to handle it, control it, use it for the advantages it offers.

To be in charge of anything we must learn to understand it and understanding the mind is, on the one hand, so beautifully simple, and on the other so frustratingly confusing, we tend to shake our heads in wonderment and go about our lives as one big question mark. There are so many different books, theories and approaches to the subject of behavioral science and identity awareness one must conclude that none has the answer. If that were not true there would be but one book or theory, and we would all use it effectively. Whether *Your Mind Can Drive You Crazy* is just another book, or whether the concepts and teachings of James A. Takacs are the ultimate answer, will depend upon your own attitude when you conclude the final chapter.

The mind, which governs the total organism and its interactions with the environment, consists of two very distinct levels, the conscious and the subconscious. It is this bi-level ''receiver'' which processes our daily input of data.

Let me share with you a rather clear explanation of the separation between these conscious and subconscious segments. A psychologist friend of mine who has devoted years to the study of hypno-therapy once offered a somewhat schematic analogy which produced an interesting mental picture of the mind.

Imagine the upper portion of the mind as the conscious level, under which lies the subconscious. Between the two, picture a tightly woven screen. Each bit of information our mind receives goes into the conscious level, passes through this screen and is lodged permanently in our subconscious. Most of this subconscious input goes unnoticed. If we are engaged in conversation the words we ''hear'' are recorded consciously, but the birds chirping in the background and the car backfiring down the street pass unnoticed by our conscious mind. Those sounds are however, shunted to our lower level and faithfully recorded. My friend suggests that in a highly relaxed state (which we shall learn is the alpha brain-wave state), this tightly woven screen also relaxes, the screen mesh separating and allowing the subconscious information to filter back up into the conscious level. This is the source of our dreams, as an example. While our conscious mind will ponder why we dreamed of a car backfiring and birds chirping, since we do not recall those incidents, we know the information was indeed there. The subconscious records *everything*, and this permanent data is the source of the mind's power.

Now let me introduce you to your tour guide for this journey into your own potential.

James A. Takacs is founder and executive director of Psychonetix, Inc., a Tarzana, California-based educational organization active in the field of individual potential development and identity awareness. Takacs (pronounced Tack-us) comes from a background of behavioral science, self-hypnosis and degrees in history, oriental languages and religion. He holds Executive Assistant and Associative Science degrees in business, has studied at Yale University in New Haven where he received his B.A., holds a Masters in history, a D.D. from Ohio Christian College and attended Sophia University in Tokyo.

Takacs attributes his military experience as the beginning of his interest in the behavioral sciences. Trained by the Air Force Institute in thought control and mass hypnosis, he was assigned to a study group ordered by President Eisenhower to investigate why captured American servicemen had succumbed to intensive mind conditioning.

For the past sixteen years Takacs has been active in his present field, conducting hundreds of lecture-seminars on many aspects of the human potential.

Although some of the information contained in this book is drawn from many different seminars on various subjects, the bulk of the text is a direct result of what has become known as the "Alpha Workshop," a series of highly refined, high intensity lecture and process seminars which grew out of Takacs' total experience in the field. The seminars at present encompass four days; Thursday and Friday evenings and full sessions Saturday and Sunday.

The "Alpha Workshop" takes its name from the state of

relaxation one attains through what is, in effect, a form of self-hypnosis. There is nothing mysterious about this "alpha" brainwave state, and we all enter it many times during the day as we drive the freeways or watch television.

These brain waves are easily measured on scientific instruments, as witness the electroencephalogram (EEG). We can clearly see on the paper graph from the EEG an actual pattern of the conscious-state "beta" wave, and as the subject relaxes, a lessening of the frequency to roughly the ten cycles per second "alpha" state. It is in this relaxed, alpha state that our subconscious lies exposed for us to examine and actually transform.

Takacs is not a guru, seer or prophet. He would be the first to refuse such a role, in fact his purpose is to free his students from *any* outside manipulation and, instead, return to them through a heightened awareness, complete mastery of their own life. He makes but one promise and it is one he is adamant about: *"Once you have completed the Alpha Workshop, you will never again have to leave your life to chance."*

In upcoming chapters you will learn we have become accustomed in our conditioning to functioning from our conscious mind level, and that this represents only 12% of our potential, the other 88% of our potential lying in the subconscious.

If you were asked to describe the nation's largest reserve of energy you would probably begin thinking of our underground oil reserves, our natural gas supply, or the un-tapped potential of atomic power generation. If you give each barrel of oil a number, each cubic yard of natural gas a number, and each un-generated kilowatt of power a number, *all* those numbers could be absorbed by the human mind. Regardless of how many millions upon millions of units, if all that data could somehow be fed to your perceptive senses, your mind would absorb it all! The *mind* itself is a tremendous, un-tapped source of energy.

Unfortunately the average person is so caught up in the daily mechanics of living, the bread-winning job responsibilities, household and child rearing duties, little time is taken to stand back and examine this reserve potential. We go through life accepting our resentments, angers, frustrations and failures as part of our destiny, part of the human condition. You are about to learn this is not true.

If you have an open mind, ready for new information and new ways of examining old information . . .

If you believe there is still much to learn about the human potential and our inherent powers . . .

If you want to at least examine what appears to be a positive, life-altering experience . . .

If, although you are now content with your attitudes and how they affect your life, you can still reach out and test new ideas . . .

Then, by all means, read on.

Finally, what you are about to read are excerpts taken from tape-recorded seminar sessions given by Psychonetix founder James A. Takacs. Much of the information is paraphrased and re-structured. In actual seminar form, with the use of blackboards, processes and visual demonstrations, the method of presenting the material is considerably altered. Where an example is given as a direct reply to a question, rather than pose both question and answer, the reply is framed in narrative form.

These then are the concepts and teachings of a rather remarkable individual—James A. Takacs.

Mel Baldwin

Chapter 1

The Conscious and Subconscious Mind

The human mind is the most complicated, sophisticated, versatile and powerful data bank in existence.

Feeding this tremendous vault of information are various senses, i.e. touch, smell, auditory, visual and memories of past sensations which involve all of these. Every day we process some 600,000 bits of such information, usually in the form of words, since that is our form of communication. During a normal day we utilize approximately 24,000 words to communicate our thoughts, only a small fraction of our daily input.

The conscious mind deals with our awareness. That's what "conscious" means; we are aware. Our conscious mind functions totally out of awareness for that is its single characteristic. It is however only 12% of our total mentality. For the average person this means 88% of one's mental capabilities remains un-tapped . . . unused. If we were told to build a house and limited to only 12% of the required material we would refuse the task, and yet we go about making our decisions with no more than that meager reserve of information to guide us.

The human consciousness has six basic functions. First, it provides the "eyes" for your intellect, the "eyes" of your mind. By eyes, I am not referring simply to the visual, I am also talking about perception. Perception means that you reach outside your physical intellect and you "perceive." You take in an idea and you change it into a mental picture, storing it in your mind. Thus, you perceive with your conscious mind.

Second: Your conscious mind is the "voice." It is the communicator for your mind. When you think, you do so in your own voice, not someone else's. The words you use are the vehicles, the communicators, the instruments for conveying ideas and thoughts, not only to the outer world, but to the inner world of your own subconscious. Incidentally, 600,000 bits of verbal data recorded by your mind daily is a deadly barrage which sometimes becomes lethal. You see, you are communicating ideas for both good *and* bad, and the words you use have a very definite effect upon your life. Since our subconscious is the wellspring from which we draw all that we use to function, it is important to use caution in what we store there.

Third: In your conscious mind you have what is called the "critical faculty." Translation: your "thinker/filter." Anytime you analyze, criticize, calculate, come to a conclusion or make a judgment, reject or accept, you do it with your critical faculty. Your critical faculty's sole job is to think/filter. When you decide what to eat, what to buy, when to add or subtract or make any decision, you are using the conscious mind. It provides all the judgments you make, but remember it can only think/filter.

Four: The will. "Will power" does not exist, per se. It is a misnomer. Although we hear much about will power, believe me, there "ain't no such animal!" Will exists on its own accord and means nothing more than the power to initiate. When an event concludes and it is time for you to go . . . to make your move, will is simply your initiator. The decisions you make are passed on to the will and the will implements them.

Five: The conscious mind is the vessel, the container for the personality. It is important to stress this point. The conscious mind is not the personality, merely the container. The reason personalities vary is the varying shapes of the individual containers. If you take a cup and fill it with coffee, the coffee will take the shape of the cup. If you pour the coffee into a vase, it will take the shape of the vase. If you want a personality that is well shaped, then you should be certain the container, your conscious mind, is shaped as you wish it.

Six: Finally we have the voluntary body functions. These are controlled by the conscious mind. I could tell you to raise your arm, to stand or to leave and you could do all these things consciously. You control the "outer shell," the large muscles. Now, if I tell you to stop digesting your meal, you would look at me like I was crazy because you cannot stop that process. Neither can you lower your blood pressure or decrease the flow of blood. You can't do it *consciously*.

Consciously you perform many functions, but they are voluntary. You exercise your critical faculty and you do what it is you have decided. This is the conscious mind and there is nothing more to it.

Somewhere along the line in the creation of man, we took a look at all this and concluded, "Well now, what we have here looks to me like a pretty good boss!" So we have come to label this conscious mind our "Boss." Your intellect becomes your boss. It can see ideas and images and impressions. It has the voice, morning, noon and night, to criticize and make all sorts of conclusions, true and false. It has the will to start anything and finish it. It has the personality to give it color and style. It controls the body functions to put it all together and make us a physical, living thing. But there is an essential ingredient missing. These six categories which we call our "boss" do not have *power!*

This tiny portion of our brain we call the conscious mind goes through life yakking a mile a minute, shouting orders in every direction, but has no power of its own. The power is vested in our subconscious. It is as quiet as the night sky with no need to have its power verified by what we do or think. Its most salient characteristic is that it operates from unawareness. It doesn't tell you, "Hey Boss, I got that information," it just goes quietly about its job of recording ... performing all its functions.

The subconscious mind is so vast that most learned men who deal in psychiatry and psychology readily admit that we know only a tiny bit about this huge part of our mind, this 88% which makes up the balance of your intellect.

Most people go through their entire lives ignoring the fact the subconscious even exists, and they do so willingly. They function on only one of their eight cylinders and wonder why things are so quiet or why they seem to be locked into a caged life-pattern and cannot escape. Like an iceberg, the human mind shows only its tip. The balance is hidden out of sight, quiet, dark and ever obedient. Anytime the conscious mind opens its mouth and says something, the subconscious picks it up and files it away. That's its job, and it does it perfectly.

The subconscious is your power source. It is the

source that keeps you functioning. It is pure power. If you live for eight hundred years you will never burn it out. It is inexhaustible.

Let's look at some every day situations. Let's say Helen comes home from the office after a day of running herself ragged. She can't wait to get home, but must add to her misery by spending an hour in the supermarket fighting crowds and bulky packages. Her conscious mind informs her she is exhausted. She gets home and is almost too tired to eat, thinking only of a warm bath and a good night's rest. Just as she is winding up the clock, her hair up and make-up off, the phone rings and it is Mr. Wonderful. She has been plotting and scheming for months to go out with this Prince Charming but so far has had nary a tumble.

Now, at twenty minutes to ten, he invites her out for a late night snack. Immediately she forgets how tired she is. Although in the morning it takes her an hour to make herself beautiful, in just twenty minutes she is standing in front of her apartment, radiant and flushed with excitement! That kind of power has to come from someplace!

Take a man in the same situation who has worked hard all day. He has put in thirty hours of overtime that week and tells his wife he just wants a TV dinner, a quick scan of the headlines and then to bed. He drags himself to the phone when it rings to discover his buddy has two free tickets to the boxing matches! He is ready in minutes and by three in the morning he is re-capping the fight over a stein of beer with his friends. By four o'clock he's back home and making amorous advances toward his wife. Now where does all that power come from? It comes from the subconscious mind, the reservoir of all our potential. The subconscious mind is your power source. Everything emanates from it.

The fact that this power source is infinite, can never wear out and can be utilized is missed by most people. Neither do they realize this power source begins operating three months after conception . . . not birth, conception. The mind is one of the first things to develop in the embryo and it keeps functioning until ten to fifteen minutes after cardiac arrest. Volunteer terminal patients have undergone exhaustive tests, and brainwave readings show that this subconscious energy continues for a period after "death." The conscious mind decays quickly and is gone. Take away anyone's oxygen and they are gone in three minutes, but the subconscious is still there, throbbing along.

So, three months after conception the light goes on and it starts humming. It becomes a living thing . . . the power source.

The subconscious mind is your storage facility. Most people are amazed when I tell them everything that has come into range of their senses since three months after conception is recorded indelibly. What you had for dinner on July 4th, 1960 is still in your memory. So is the person you sat with and all the conversation which ensued.

Your first day of school is equally indelibly imprinted in your subconscious mind, as are all the student's names, your teacher—everything. So too is your moment of birth, with all its attendant pain, frustration, strangeness, confusion, etc. There is no limit to the subconscious mind's ability to store information. If you could study for 200 years, day and night, the sum total of all that knowledge and information would be like a tiny marble inside the Houston Astrodome. You will never fill up those brain cells—never—there are just too many of them.

The human mind is the most fascinating piece of machinery in the world. Every night as you sleep, some

50,000 brain cells are destroyed through normal attrition, yet they pass on stored data to 50,000 new brain cells which you regenerate to take their place! The brain's ability to electro-chemically function and record is almost beyond our comprehension.

There is one facet of the brain's abilities which can prove to be man's bane or his boon, depending upon how the person deals with it, and it is this: Everything that comes into range of your senses is date-stamped the moment it is received. This is extremely important. The subconscious date-stamps it and makes a clear impression of it, then stores it away permanently.

Let's say you are three years old and sitting in your high-chair eating creamed spinach. You are not only eating it, but you're wearing it, smeared all over your face, having a ball giggling and splashing the spinach with your spoon. Just then mommy's apron catches fire and she screams horribly in a moment of intense panic. This impression is lodged in your subconscious along with the taste and texture of the spinach. Somehow the mind comes to the conclusion the two go together. Forty years later you still cannot "stomach" the sight of spinach because it was date-stamped and impressed upon your subconscious along with mommy's near disaster.

A great deal of human suffering is caused by this idiotic association of ideas imprinted in the subconscious which supplies the power to the conscious mind. You are an expression of your subconscious, and your aversion to mice or green beans or what-have-you is tied to some incident in your past which made a negative impression on your subconscious. Mice or green beans are associated with that incident.

One man I worked with could not stand the sight,

sound or smell of onions. They actually made him ill. He had his poor wife running. She had to turn over his hamburger with a spatula which had not touched onions. She had to barbecue her own outside because he could not even tolerate the smell and would raise the roof if he so much as spied an onion in the kitchen.

In my living room, while he was under hypnosis, I gave him a Spanish onion and said, "Here is a delicious Washington apple. Eat it." He began to eat the "apple," even leaving a "core," and we know there is no core in an onion. Furthermore, I told him that when he awakened, he would have the taste of cloves in his mouth and he would feel good for having eaten that Washington apple. His wife, of course, was horror stricken. I cautioned her to keep this secret for two weeks ... not to tell him his "apple" was indeed a dreaded onion.

Two weeks later she called to say she had finally told him about the incident and he had promptly become ill. Now an onion is long lasting, but not two weeks! By then his system would have disposed of it. His subconscious had listened well, and for two weeks he felt no ill effects. Then, his conscious mind was informed of the incident and he made himself ill.

Your likes and dislikes are all rooted in the subconscious and they are all date-stamped. If you encounter someone about whom you note a trait that is very definitely childish and immature, recognize the fact that person is operating on a three-year-old's date-stamped memory impression.

The subconscious is our feeling mind, the source of all that we perceive as smooth or rough, hot or cold, sad or funny, painful or pleasurable. It cannot think nor can it reason, those being the job of the conscious mind. The subconscious has no means by which to judge the merit of an idea. Since all it can do is feel, it is the source of our emotions—all of them. When you "feel," the subconscious passes the impression on to the conscious mind and you then register it in your awareness.

Here is something which surprises most people: since it cannot think and reason, since it cannot judge merit, the only thing the subconscious mind can do is agree with you. It lacks the ability to reject. It can only nod its head and say, "Yes Boss." It has only the capacity to obey, designed by nature to be your servant.

To those in my seminar I suggest they put a sign on their bathroom mirror, to be seen every time they brush their teeth or comb their hair. That sign reads, "NEVER PERMIT YOURSELF TO SAY YOU ARE ANYTHING YOU DO NOT WANT TO BE." Should you forget this and say, "Boy am I stupid," that subconscious voice will simply say, "Yes Boss, stupid." It has all the power to do exactly what you tell it to do. If you want to be nervous, go right ahead, but don't verbalize it. If you don't want to *be* something, then don't give your subconscious the order for it will simply obey. When you say "I am tired," your subconscious agrees with the order and you become tired. Tiredness is most often mental in origin, not a physical disability. If you do not believe this, tell a pooped and drained friend he has just won the Irish Sweepstakes and watch what happens.

The subconscious has no ability to perceive. Since it can only accept the material it receives from the conscious mind, it therefore cannot differentiate between what is real and what is imagined. That is why we need exercise caution in providing it with information.

Let's examine worry. Worry is strictly the process by

which you visualize what you don't want. Your subconscious, ever obedient, only sees what it is you don't want and has no way of judging that it hasn't happened yet, so it will act accordingly. How many times have you said, "I'd better be careful or I'll drop that," only to immediately let the object fall from your fingers? Worry cripples your own creativity. If you say, "I'd like that job but probably won't get it," your subconscious will prepare your mood, your personality, your attitude and you indeed will probably not get the job.

Another example of the power resting in your subconscious can be seen in bad dreams. One of man's biggest fears is that of falling. When you dream of falling, you awaken in perspiration, trembling, your heart rate increased. These physiological changes were not brought about by the conscious mind as they would be through voluntary over-exertion. They were caused by the subconscious. Lying in bed, you have not moved an inch but your subconscious responded to the imagined dream and you physically reacted exactly as if you were actually falling.

Finally, the subconscious mind takes care of all your involuntary body functions. It is the custodian of your physical being, however your conscious mind often interrupts this care-taking duty. It is the conscious mind which implants those picky, picky thoughts of doubt, forever misdirecting the subconscious. Unfortunately, the subconscious is tied to the conscious mind and it must obey.

I am not implying we would all be happier if we had just the subconscious mind, only that it would be perfect if we could stop the conscious mind from its constant interrupting.

There is one law of life you cannot escape. The law is this: ANY IDEA YOU HOLD TO BE TRUE IS BINDING

UPON YOU. It determines the outcome of your behavior. The law does not say "every law that is true," but every idea that you *hold to be true*. It matters not the source of the idea. It could have been spoon-fed to you by your mother, father, teacher, minister, close friend or your spouse. The source is unimportant. What is important is that you hold the idea to be true. That's all the subconscious mind needs to act upon.

One lady wrote to Ann Landers and said that even though she presumed it to be a silly superstition, whenever she suffered a sty on her eyelid she rubbed it with a gold ring, and the sty went away! She asked Ann just how this could happen. Ann wrote back to say she didn't think there were any medical properties in a gold ring. You now know the answer: if you hold the idea to be true, that a gold ring will take away a sty, then it will do just that!

There are many examples of how an idea, a belief, can lead to the assumed consequence, such as: If you go outside and your hair is wet, you will catch cold. If you go swimming anytime less than an hour after eating, you will suffer cramps. It is amazing how many people are saddled with ideas that have little or no basis in truth. They are just ideas we pick up and transfer over to our obedient servant, our subconscious, which makes certain the idea is realized.

On the positive side of this ledger is the field of psychosomatic medicine. Look, if you believe smearing peanut butter on your big toe will cure dandruff, then good-bye dandruff!

A recent development in this area has come from the University of California at San Francisco where a team of researchers found that people do indeed have the ability to generate a natural pain-killing substance in their own brain. The scientists noted that when a patient was secretly given a placebo or "sugar pill," instead of a pain relieving drug, the patient appeared to stimulate his brain and pituitary gland into producing and releasing a class of compounds called "endorphins."

Scottish scientists at the University of Aberdeen first identified these endorphins in 1975. Chemically similar to compounds found in the opium poppy, their effect appears to be not unlike that of morphine, derived from the poppy. These endorphins have in fact been dubbed, "the brain's own opiate."

We are thus given the fact that certain patients who simply *believe* they are receiving a beneficial pain-killer, even when given only a "sugar pill," can themselves generate an opiate-like compound to provide their body the relief it now expects! Is it really that simple? Can an attitude cure? Yes, because we already know that an attitude can make us ill. That's where ulcers, hypertension and heart attacks come from. The body, through its own natural functions, stimulated by how we feel, react or think ... what we believe ... *can* produce actual chemical changes within its own system. This then is the power we can all use to help cure ourselves and keep our physical being in proper health. Let's add some other interesting theories or "agreements" and see what we get:

The medical "agreement" has for the most part confirmed that the body at birth is designed to last approximately two-hundred years. What we wear out, of course, are the parts. The heart, the kidneys, the lungs, the gastrointestinal tract wear out due to mal-treatment. We smoke cigarettes or live in highly polluted urban areas and we damage our lung tissue. We worry, fail to handle daily stresses and our stomach acids produce ulcers. We overtax and weaken our digestive sphincter muscles by our own reactions to outside influences and we get "up-tight." We eat improperly and cholesterol packs our arteries, disrupting normal blood flow. Our unwillingness to deal with stresses increases our blood pressure to the point where our artery walls suffer aneurysmal swelling and even burst. The list goes on and on to include almost all our essential organs.

Okay, when we have damaged tissue can we actually repair it ourselves? By getting in touch with our own physical being through alpha, can we manufacture new tissue to replace the old? Can we generate an army of white blood cells to combat infection? Can we, in the alpha state, using these energy powers, direct our cells to re-form, re-build damaged cells?

To respond to that question, let's examine this fact: When a mother, regardless of her own age, gives birth to a baby, that infant is wholly constructed of *brand new tissue*. Each cell which makes up the infant's body, the eyes, the organs, the bones, the fingernails, is brand new ... manufactured by an adult female. So, a thirty or even forty year old body *can* manufacture new cells, new tissue! (Let's adhere to the tenets of ERA and give the male the same power.)

There is obviously much re-thinking to be done before we resign ourselves to an acceptance of physical and emotional ailments, infirmities and illnesses, just because, "that's the way it is!"

Watch television. Advertisers know the susceptibility of the mind to ideas. When you are relaxed, poaching your brain before the small or wide screen, your mind is acutely receptive. You are told that the long, thin aspirin ... the green and white one ... will completely relieve your headache. If you choose to really believe this, then sure enough, that long, thin, green and white aspirin will make your headache disappear. Advertising actually aims to get you to buy a product against your better judgment. They know if they aim for the 88% of your brain rather than the 12% they have a much larger target and if they can dull your senses, get your critical faculty out of the way, it will not rise up to defend the suggestion. The idea penetrates the subconscious and you suddenly get the urge to buy a particular brand over the one you've been using.

Consider the person who wishes to stop smoking. He or she has seen horrible anti-smoking films on lung damage and associated cancer, knows full well that cigarettes are shortening the life span, and yet the habit is so strong the act of quitting is nearly impossible. Stop-smoking clinics approach the result of the problem but not the problem itself. Our conscious mind resents being denied a desire and when we subject ourselves to negative input by way of minor shock annoyances or excess conditioning, we may stop smoking briefly, but for most people it does not last. The reason is simple. A person who is by conditioning and habit a smoker, is still a smoker—he/she has simply denied the being the privilege. When one gets in tune with the subconscious and actually *becomes* a person who does not smoke, then the urge or thought about smoking does not apply to them any longer. Stopping smoking then becomes a natural consequence of a person who does not smoke!

The old saying that what you don't know won't hurt you is just not true. You cannot consciously will away a habit. You must re-educate the subconscious. I tell my students what they learned prior to attending the workshop will not serve them during the seminar. The conscious mind is not the part we deal with. In alpha or self-hypnosis we contact the subconscious and learn how to systematically feed it the ideas which will best serve us. Conscious applications of new data require some one-hundred exposures. In hypnosis only one-tenth the number is needed. Some psychiatrists contend that it takes 600 conscious exposures to equal just six applications in hypnosis.

(I use the terms alpha training and self-hypnosis interchangeably. The process for reaching the alpha brainwave level is the same for reaching a state of self-hypnosis. For this reason I will, from this point on, use the term "alpha" in this regard.)

Alpha training is not restricted to any set procedure. There are literally hundreds of ways to achieve a hypnotic "trance." Alpha is but a vehicle—a tool to be used in reaching and stimulating the subconscious. It is simply the means by which you extract your full potential.

Just learning the mechanics of alpha does not make you a successful practitioner, nor will simply reading a good book on the subject. There are many pitfalls, not dangerous mind you, just pitfalls. My job is to guide you around these and provide the background and information you require . . . instruct you in techniques that work. It is however, something you must keep using—constantly.

I do not have the power to alter your life. You do. I am not a guru. What I can do is assist you in achieving complete freedom from me and everyone else—freedom from all the things which you use to inhibit yourself. You are then free to exercise your options and gain mastery over your *own* life. I will just do my job and fulfill my promise that you never again need leave your life to chance.

As we get deeper into the subject I will begin taking

words away from you to demonstrate just how poisonous they are. You will learn the negative value of such words as "hope," "t-r-y," and "wish." You will learn to re-word and bring the conscious and subconscious into productive harmony.

If you don't like "worms" why would you talk about them with revulsion, which only reinforces your aversion? Remember you are not a single entity. You have two living mechanisms sharing the same mind. Your mind is not only in your head, since your nervous system penetrates every last organ, tissue, cell and gland in your being. You are a living mind and cannot separate the mind from the body. Any attempt to do so and both parts will die. Accept the fact the mind encompasses every part of your living being, and what affects one is surely going to affect the other.

Alpha is the vehicle with which we contact, influence and re-educate the subconscious.

Doctors recognize the fact that 90% of what comes into their offices is mind-caused. Ulcers, hardening of the arteries, migraines, asthma, high blood pressure are all psychosomatic. One physician told me he had a list of 93 diseases and illnesses which he had treated over the years and all but three were psychosomatic—mental in origin. The other three were indeed organic in nature.

Such psychosomatic illnesses are easily alleviated when you join the mind and body together, working harmoniously. You have a magnificent servant waiting to do your bidding. All you need do is get through to it in an organized way and it will do anything you ask of it.

Once you assert your absolute authority you will have mastery over your own attitudes. Let's face it, the subconscious mind has been having a picnic, taking in everything but letting old "12%" haul the entire load. You change this lazy-fat genie which has been lying back doing little, into a source of power that starts giving practical, workable orders.

It will try to horse you around because it is a living entity and your skull-mate—your alter ego. If it balks at following orders, throw a few choice words at it to get it going in the right direction. It is your feeling mind and does not like being insulted or chastised at all.

Taking charge of the conscious mind is the most rewarding result of alpha training. The conscious mind acts as an analytical screen through which ideas pass. If the incoming idea matches what is in the subconscious it will be accepted. If the idea is not compatible with what is in your memory bank, the idea is rejected. The conscious mind will spring to the defense of any previously conditioned idea, since it represents part of an existing belief system. As far as the mind is concerned, a belief is far stronger than a fact.

It is interesting to note the conscious mind was not always a part of your being. From three months after conception until approximately the age of three years, you function without the conscious mind. There is no critical faculty, no idea perception or "personality." There is certainly no "will," since the infant functions solely out of conditioning. Touch a stove: hot! You know to stay away from big metal boxes that are hot. This is part of our early responsive conditioning.

Many parents decide to have their arguments when the child is napping, assuming he will thus be uninvolved. The child, however, is just as receptive then as when he is wide awake since the subconscious faithfully logs all the shouting and anger.

Let's consider a tiny baby, just born and quietly

sleeping in the maternity ward nursery, comfortable and warm. In runs an excited Greek grandmother. It is her first grandchild and despite her dinner celebration of too much Greek wine and lots of garlic, she wants to nuzzle the new offspring. She picks up the baby and as only an emotional Greek grandmother can do, she begins hugging the tiny child, covering it with kisses. The nurse, alarmed, rushes in and attempts to retrieve the baby. The nurse is pulling in one direction, the grandmother in another, amid screaming and garlic scented shouts of protest. The infant, in a matter of seconds, has been forced from his quiet napping into a world of erratic movement and loud confusion.

Next to falling, the strongest fear we develop as children is the fear of loud noises, and here we have an infant in the midst of raucous confusion. The incident is immediately date-stamped and implanted in the child's subconscious. Forty years later, as an adult, he or she can have a strong aversion to foreign accents, garlic, wine, white uniforms, hospitals ... a whole array of different negatives, all labeled "bad."

Nature provides roughly 3 years and 6 months of absolute and total dominance over the life of a child. From 3 until around 10 you will have an approximate 30% growth in the conscious mind. This is when the personality begins to develop. He starts yelling, "No, I won't do it," stamping his foot. He begins to figure things out for himself instead of asking mommy ... begins to tinker, experiment and thus learn. He is now thinking and analyzing, talking freely and making pretty good sense. He begins to perceive ideas. He starts relating stories with, "Mommy, guess what I saw?" So here, we have 30% growth.

Now, from the age of 10 to about the age of 17, you

have the largest percentage of growth, an additional 60 or
so to add to the other 30%. Note that the largest part of
growth comes during the teen years. Teenagers are growing psychologically as well as physically and organically.
Here is where we find the greatest struggle for identity,
searching for a purpose. They have 8-million questions
and want them all answered at once. They begin making
decisions for themselves, some workable and most un-
workable. They begin looking further down the road and
stop playing to become involved in the work ethic.

Finally, from 17 to about 25, nature puts on the last
10% of the polish, the final coat, and for better or for
worse, this sealer goes on and the conscious mind becomes
firm.

We now have a totally formed personality, an emotional and physical oneness. We have a person who may
indeed express a strong distaste for wine, Greeks and
nurses' uniforms, an aversion to mice and moths, a person
who is traumatized by large crowds or elevators or heights.
All the data is imprinted and is simply offered up on
demand.

The entire purpose of alpha training is to lull the
conscious mind to one side where it can no longer spring
up to defend against implanted ideas. It is then we can
transform the negative ideas into positive ideas that will
nurture and support us. We must recognize and appreciate
the sheer power of our subconscious and convert it to
positive use.

When I think of this power, and how unaware we are
of how it functions, I recall the words of a physician. The
late Dr. C. Landry Cooper of Hollywood was an excellent
general practitioner in that he was keenly attuned to the art
of diagnostic medicine.

A friend of mine, bothered by chronic heartburn for some ten or twelve years was told about Dr. Cooper by a devoted patient. Having spent a considerable sum on three experts in internal medicine, my friend decided to not only visit Dr. Cooper, but admitted he did so with a challenge. In effect he said, "You're supposed to be so smart, cure me of my heartburn!"

The doctor was very matter of fact, stating that the medical knowledge of diagnostics was sufficient to locate the problem and either alleviate it or cure it, if it was indeed physical.

After a considerable series of tests, barium swallows, x-rays and probing, my friend was called back for the report. Holding up the x-rays, the doctor pointed to all of the areas of the digestive system controlled by the sphincter muscles. In each case it was proven these muscles were so tightly gathered that the normal flow of food intake was interrupted. Whereas the esophagus should have disposed of the barium after a prescribed period of time, x-rays showed the barium still locked tightly above the sphincter at its base. The same held true for passages into and out of the upper and lower intestines as well as the colon. It was determined by Dr. Cooper that while my friend was organically in perfect condition—the vital organs passing with flying colors—physiologically he was a mess!

"Can you cure me?" my friend asked. "No," said the doctor, "unless we could determine the reason why you're all tensed up! If I knew it was because your mother-in-law was living with you and I could get her to move, then I could cure it!"

Dr. Cooper then offered a hypothetical case, as follows:

A man comes home from a pleasant day at the office,

is met by a charming wife who is well coiffed and delightfully dressed. A kiss on the cheek and he is led to his favorite easy chair, his shoes exchanged for slippers, a sports page and a cocktail handed him to enjoy before dinner. As he sits there the scent of a seven-bone roast wafts under his nose and while it is not registered by his conscious mind, which is heavy into the baseball scores, his subconscious files it away and starts directing the involuntary machinery of the body.

"Okay you guys," it says, "let's start cranking out some digestive juices down there, old Harvey's got a huge roast to handle, probably with starchy potatoes, maybe more pepper than he should have. Okay salivary glands, let's get the saliva started," the subconscious continues, "lots of chewing coming up!"

While Harvey sits there, his physical body is already preparing for his meal. His mouth begins watering, his sphincters begin relaxing in preparation and his stomach is chemically ready for digestion.

Harvey goes to the table, set with candles and crystal, and begins an enjoyable meal with a warm and smiling companion.

Suddenly the door bursts open and in pops your friendly neighborhood gun-in-hand burglar, demanding, "Gimme all your money!" In an instant Harvey's physical system completely changes. The shock starts a chain reaction.

The mind dredges up all the necessary fears to start severe trauma. Gun equals death, robbery equals loss, the simple unknown equals fear! The mind starts a whole series of new directives:

"Hey, stomach," it shouts, "pump in ten times more acid, this guy's in trouble! More adrenalin!"

Harvey's mouth turns dry, his sphincters grab on for dear life, food is stopped where it sits, his muscular peristaltic action, the wave-like movement which forces food in the proper direction, stops and in severe shock can actually reverse itself and cause regurgitation.

Doctor Cooper's point was clear. In a fraction of a second Harvey has been changed from a perfectly functioning system into one which is literally a mess! And Harvey had nothing to do with it. His mind did it!

Remember, you are the living expression of your subconscious mind, since your subconscious is the mind and body combined. Everything you do is predicated upon your 88% vault. The way you walk, talk, eat, write or shake hands cannot be duplicated by anyone else for it is the sum total of your own store of information.

Now let's get a closer look at the critical faculty. This, remember, is our "thinker/filter" with which we ponder, judge and decide. The critical faculty is the one which causes all the mayhem since long before your day of awareness of the existence of the subconscious/conscious mind, you have already developed ideas. As proven before, they become implanted firmly in that 3-months to 3-years period and the 3 to 17-years period. For you parents who might be concluding there's not much you can do with the young child when all these motivating ideas are already implanted, let me assure you that is untrue.

Nature, in her wisdom in structuring all this, did not leave parents helpless with no recourse, and the solution I am going to give you will probably test your incredulity.

Each day in the life of the child seventeen or younger, there is a period of time when his 88% data bank is totally open for business—the first hour of sleep. During this time, parents who are properly trained may do all their instructing, the programming which is desirable.

This particular exercise has transformed entire families. Although some parents find it uncomfortable at first, their conscious mind throwing up thoughts like, "this is ridiculous," or "Jim's got to be kidding," it does, however, work.

To accomplish this, I train not only the parents, but also the children with the parents. They take the programs home with them and adapt them to their living pattern. Parents wait until the youngster is naturally asleep and sometime during that first hour they sit near the child and repeat, over and over, "You are smart, you are extremely clever and school becomes easier and easier because school is something you fully enjoy."

Now, the child cannot argue with this information because his judgmental critical faculty is out-to-lunch. The child is now completely open and receptive. The new and constructive attitude toward his learning ability and school is gradually implanted smack in the midst of his distaste for spinach, Greeks, grandmothers, garlic and hospitals. Regardless what the child says when he is awake, he can be programmed beautifully during that first hour of sleep.

The Alpha Workshop focuses for the most part on the transformation of the adult mind. We take the conscious mind, push it aside and expose the subconscious. Adults have a very hard-core critical faculty since it consists of all the facts, figures, nonsense and old wives' tales they pick up during their life. This critical faculty will immediately challenge any new idea and instantly refute it, since its own source of information is all the stored garbage of life.

If I tell a non-hypnotized subject who is overweight, "You are slender," she will rise to the suggestion with protest. "Are you crazy," she shouts, "just look at me! I can look in the mirror! I can see what I am! I am fat!'' Do you hear what she is telling herself? Do you see how her past garbage rises to attack the new idea?

Take the same woman and put her in alpha, and she cannot defend her fat belief since her conscious critical faculty is shunted aside. The idea of "slender" goes right into the subconscious and if continually reapplied she begins to automatically create "slender" and not "fat." Without even being aware of it, her attitude changes . . . her eating habits change . . . and finally the thin-thought becomes so much stronger than the fat-thought she finds herself actually losing weight! This happens because, as I said before, your physical being is a direct and living expression of your subconscious being. People who have in the past considered, "You are what you think," begin to see it as not just an old cliché, but an actual fact.

That is what hypnosis or alpha training is all about. We develop the ability to lull the conscious mind into stepping aside and we then feed the subconscious the ideas we want it to give back to us physically and emotionally.

Some students ask whether it might be just as easy to consciously re-program the subconscious. The answer is based upon information I have already given you, in that six sessions of hypnotic suggestion equal six-hundred conscious applications. Unfortunately most people do not have the time or stamina to stick with such a lengthy conscious program, especially when it is unnecessary. With each alpha training session there are ninety-nine conscious-state sessions which become unnecessary. It's simple mathematics.

Chapter 2

Our Human Emotions

Many of our emotions are what I call natural hypnotizers. They not only feed the mind, they give it a royal banquet. Often the mind is so busy devouring these strong emotional entrees it shuts everything else down completely. In such instances we sometimes find the person completely incapacitated. Let's examine some of these emotions.

Fear: This is one capable of jamming aside your conscious mind and without thinking, if someone yells "fire" you will crawl, jump or run out of the building without caring whether it's the first or tenth floor. You will do this regardless of how weak or tired you are, you *move!* The critical mind is shoved aside with no chance to say, "Forget it, you're tired." No, you're on the tenth floor and you are going to get out even if it means leaping from the window.

Fear is not only one of the strongest influences on the mind, it breeds many other emotions in its wake.

Anger: This one doesn't bother with shades of grey, it appears in living black and red. You can actually reach out and touch it. It shows you the true power of hypnosis. In its

25

strongest form we call it "blind rage" and that word "blind" is your clue. Is he reasonable? No. And man, is he strong! He threw the couch right out the window!

Anger triggers all the past garbage to make itself known. Listen to a heated argument; "Ten years ago he borrowed my fishing rod and broke it and didn't even offer to pay for it!" Suddenly all the old, pent-up personal affronts are dredged up to feed the anger. People in the heat of anger always bring up matters which have nothing to do with the current situation. It's obviously because your tormentor is a person who eats garlic! Who else would shout at you the wáy he did! How dare he!

Here is where the subconscious really scrapes the bottom of the barrel, feeding your mind with bad feelings a mile-a-minute. You can't figure out why, in your struggle to gain control, you're saying all these things. Why do you want to lash out and hurt this person? The feelings are so strong people actually vibrate. You will never see any indication of calmness in a raging person.

When the matter is settled we deal then with remorse and wonder. "Did I really say all those things?" When they say they cannot remember, they are not pulling your leg. It was the subconscious which fed all that past-hurt data.

Hunger: You have just finished a full-course dinner and are sitting with friends over a final cup of coffee. You are completely satiated . . . that last bite of steak really packed you full . . . you cannot even think about another bite.

Suddenly the pastry cart rolls by and everyone begins selecting a choice dessert. So you take one and devour it heartily. Why in the world would you eat if your stomach is actually full? Because you do not think of hunger, you only think of past pastry delights and the tasty association rules the situation. The food itself goes right past your critical faculty, your judgmental ability, and you eat the dessert.

Overweight people attempting to diet will tell you in nauseating detail the number of times they have robbed the refrigerator against their "will." Reason doesn't count for anything. Something *else* is driving them to over-eat and that something else is lodged in their subconscious. They can only deal with it when they know what it is and reprogram the data.

Thirst: Consider a motorist in the Mojave desert. He stops for a glass of water, then drives a few more miles down a seldom traveled road where his car engine blows up. He gets out in the hot sun, looks at all that desert sand and what is the first thing that pops into his mind? Thirst! People die of dehydration in remote deserts! One must have water to survive! Before he takes his first step he is thirsty, even though he has just fully quenched that thirst a few miles back. Desert, thirst, water and thirst, the cycle is repeated. Whereas his body water-content is then sufficient to provide the energy to walk the necessary distance, his mind takes over and tells him he won't make it. Finally, a mile or two later, he has bombarded his subconscious mind so much with thirst and water, the subconscious obeys and says, "OK, you can have it," and projects into his conscious mind a mirage, an oasis in the desert. The mirage is not caused by heat waves, but by the subconscious obeying the command which he has hammered into his mind—water—water—water. Oddly enough the mirage is usually familiar looking. It may become the A & W Rootbeer stand from his own neighborhood, or perhaps the lake he frequented as a child. Whatever he sees is familiar because its source is his memory bank, his storage bin of places or photographs of his past. His mind's "eye" actually sees it, and even though his reasoning tells him it is not really there, he may actually rip off his clothes and jump into the sand anyway.

Hate: Here is a word we use inappropriately and recklessly. A minor discomfort or distaste is more easily rejected if we are motivated by hate. Hate is the conscious mind's handiest emotion for rejecting an idea not compatible with our stored garbage. "I hate cauliflower . . . I hate that person . . . I hate to fly." Come on now. Hate? Remember, any idea we hold to be true is binding upon us, and when we condition our subconscious with that verbal expression of "hate," it is exactly the emotion we feel.

Knowing just this one fact can open us up to actually dealing with minor distastes or annoyances and we can easily transform ourselves . . . learn to understand and accept the "hated" person, or learn to enjoy flying, or at least eat cauliflower without bitching about it.

Love: Both hate and love are hypnotics. There is an old saying you cannot reason with a man in love, and that anyone who hates will continue to do so with no regard for reason, knowledge, religion or even good intentions. Nothing interferes with that hatred or with love.

Arm yourself with undeniable proof and tell a man his current lady friend is no good. He will knock your block off! Defend someone that person hates, and when his hate turns to rage against you, run!

The full gamut of our emotions has within it the power to produce improper or unreasonable behavior, even to completely incapacitate us.

Boredom: This is a good one. Boredom is actually a subtle form of anger and it drives people to do all sorts of things. How many times have you done something you later regretted, out of sheer boredom?

Need: Here is one that can produce a beneficial end result when accurately defined and channeled properly, but more often it causes us to focus on what isn't rather than what is. This is the source of discontent. Disappointment is most often the result of an unrealistic expectation.

Guilt: One of the strongest mental debilitators, this one is the poison of our personality. Guilt is the one emotion which kills more people than any other and one we will examine more closely later on.

Fervor: Political or religious, any type of fervor is hypnotic, for it drives out reason and replaces it with emotion.

Monotony: Although akin to boredom, monotony has its own causative power. Music comes under the heading of monotony. They call it mood music and you can listen to it for an hour and not actually hear anything. Haven't you ever put on an album, softly playing as you rest, only to be alerted to the scratching sound of the needle in the final groove? The "mood" music has passed the conscious level and you have been with your own thoughts in an alpha-nap.

Every single day you pass through these states of receptivity when your subconscious mind is exposed. As mentioned earlier, freeway driving produces alpha, as does television. Television is the perfect solution for the monotony of a lazy mind. The movie is on film and the film consists of individual frames which pass by at so many frames-per-second, each one a tiny impulse that beats on the eye's retina, causing retinal fatigue. If the film is of sufficient interest or value, you fight this fatigue and enjoy the program's content. If it is less than interesting, you find yourself becoming sleepy and it is simply retinal fatigue.

Fatigue: This one is also a hypnotizer. It is not only physical as in post-exercise, it is mental as well. (Being tired is not the same as being fatigued, incidentally. Physical fatigue carries with it the sense of expended physical energy.) When you ram into the conscious mind so many impulses or bits of information that the poor thing is struggling to grasp it all, you suffer mental fatigue. Both are potential debilitators.

Tiredness is not always a lack of Geritol's iron in the blood. It is only a developed comfort habit of the mind, as witness the young lady rising to the late-night occasion to meet Mr. Wonderful.

Remember, our emotions are the products of our subconscious mind, not the conscious level. Our conscious mind can only serve us a meal of emotions if it gets the raw ingredients from our memory bank, and thus the only way we can alter a negative emotion is to get inside the subconscious and understand or transform the raw product data.

Chapter 3

The Words We Use

In commenting earlier on communication, we acknowledged that words were the source of our thoughts and imagery. When someone says "book," we not only imagine the shape and size of an object, but we most often visualize the word b-o-o-k.

Words our conscious mind speaks or thinks are highly descriptive, with each word having two distinct functions. One is the word's definition, the other is its connotation.

Definition is simply the meaning of any word. We define the word until we know what *it* means (a judgment of our critical faculty) and then use that word in the future to describe what *we* mean. We use the word's definition to get our point across. Remember, this is all a process of our analyzer, our conscious mind.

The connotation of a word, on the other hand, is the meaning of the word, *plus* the emotional impact of the word. This being the case, which part of our mind are we now using? Right, the subconscious, the non-thinker, the one which can only bow and say, "Yes Boss."

As we progress in our examination of words, you will find us dealing less with definitions and more with connotations, since we focus on the subconscious "feeling mind" and not the conscious critical faculty.

Here's how nature has us set up: An idea pops into our mind, into our conscious awareness, and it is immediately transmitted to the subconscious as an image. The subconscious, being blind, has no ability to perceive. It just takes the impression you hand it. It does one other thing, however, and this is extremely important: it adds to the word an emotional impact. We now have not just the definition of the word, but a connotation of it. The image is now produced by the subconscious and (remember, it uses the physical body) we get it back as an *attitude*. (To prove our subconscious uses the physical body, just show a woman a vampire bat and watch her face and where she places her hands.)

Since this is important, let's retrace that path again: An idea is conceived at the conscious level and is defined. It is passed to the subconscious where it is logged and given an emotion. The word or idea is then passed back to our conscious mind with the addition of an attitude.

I say this is important because it shows us clearly that the only way we are going to alter a negative attitude is to get into our subconscious memory bank and re-program the data it uses to create our attitudes! *When we change the idea we implant in our subconscious, the attitude associated with that idea automatically changes.*

If you associate with any of us who work at The Centre, our Psychonetix office building, there is one word you will rarely, if ever, hear. That word is T-R-Y. If it is used by one of our staff it is always spelled aloud and not spoken. T-R-Y is the most poisonous word in the English language.

I said I would assist you in deleting words from your everyday conversations, and T-R-Y is the first on our list.

"Try," by definition, means to make an effort, to attempt, to endeavor. We do not quarrel with the definition, only the connotation, and in this area "try" is deadly.

Three things can occur in the subconscious: First, it programs us for failure. "If at first you don't succeed, try, try again." If "try" means to succeed, why are there *two* "trys" in that quotation? "She tried thirty-nine times and finally gave up." "I tried to quit smoking but failed." "I tried to lose weight but failed." "I tried to be a good mother but failed."

Failure is implicitly transmitted in the image of the word "try." The instruction of failure is thus implanted in our subconscious mind, not as a definition, but as a connotation. It is what the word really "means," when we add an emotion to the definition.

With this now programmed in our mind, our goal seeking mechanism in our computer accepts the continual "try, try, try," as the goal . . . a goal to fail. Just when you're about to make it, something goes wrong, everything falls apart and you wonder why you're "trying" so hard! It fell apart because that's the way you had it programmed. You created the space for yourself to just "try." You didn't say you'd *do* it! You only said you'd "try."

Secondly, "try" is wholly negative. Let's examine why. Life, to be lived fully, requires total commitment. When we maintain that commitment we lead full and happy lives. Putting out less than our all is the source of much of our unhappiness . . . much of our guilt.

"Try" is by its very nature the ultimate cop-out. It enables us to escape responsibility for not doing something. It's amazing how much we can hide behind so small a word. "Try" is completely debilitating for it keeps us from saying yes or no . . . making a commitment. Yes and no are hot or cold words, but "try" is always lukewarm. When you say "I'll try," your subconscious files it under "fail" and says "Yes, Boss," and the program for failure is complete.

If you examine people you know who are chronic "try" users, you will invariably find they are also the most failure oriented and the most frustrated. They do not seem to have the power to achieve their goals so they remain stuck somewhere between desire and fulfillment.

You invite a friend to a party and she says, "I'll try." Let's say it's a surprise party so time is important. You stress that she should be there at 8 o'clock. "I'll try," is still her answer. Do yourself a favor and don't plan on her being there at eight, or ever. There was no commitment made, no "Yes, I'll be there!" When your expected guest says "try," you yourself automatically flash on the negative feeling implicit in the word and must honestly admit you really don't expect her to appear. There's no commitment, none whatsoever. It's that lukewarm middle ground that leaves everyone up in the air . . . air filled with such emotions as disappointment, misery, anger, frustration and on the part of the perpetrator, guilt.

Thirdly, "try" is inconvertible. Imagine sitting at your desk, leaning back for a moment, lost in your thoughts, or just enjoying a "nothing" break. Suddenly I rush up to you and say, "Try!" What will your reaction or answer be? You will be puzzled. Try what? What are you talking about? Dial the phone? Stand up? What should I do? Be specific!

Your mind's processor can't handle "try" as a directive. It can handle "sing" or "walk" or "talk," "sit up," "run," "eat," but it can't handle "try." It's a matter of specificity.

When your mind comes across "try" it's like getting a mouthful of lukewarm water. What does it do with it? It can't analyze it . . . it will simply spiral it back inward in what we call frustration. People who "try" hardest are always the most frustrated and they do it to themselves. They set up the program . . . they build the cage from which they seek to escape.

If nothing else I say to you sticks, then at least get a firm hold on this. Do yourself a favor and get rid of this word. Take "try" out of your vocabulary. It doesn't mean anything. It's over-used and mis-used. If I tell you to try and pick up a chair, you will proudly and promptly pick up a chair, and yet I did not ask that of you. If I had wanted the chair picked up I would have said "pick up the chair." I only said "*try* to pick up the chair." Other than associating "try" with "fail" your mind has all kinds of trouble with it. Toss it out!

A number of things happen when you delete "try" from your vocabulary. First, you stop pushing your own failure button. Instead of going down that long road to failure, you get off it. Now you at least have an alternative. Secondly, you become more decisive. You must now actually commit yourself to your own life and stop abdicating your responsibility.

Someone says, "Can you make it?" You say, "Yes, I'll be there," or "No, I cannot be there." If you have genuine doubt, not based on indecision but perhaps on an airliner arrival, then if you really want to be there you can say, "I'll do my best to be there." Nobody is going to demand more of you than your best, so if you don't show up they'll know there was adequate reason for your absence.

Finally, since "try" is inconvertible, you are now going to have to say what it is you really mean. You may use the word "strive" if you must, since it does mean you are going forward, putting your full energies into it, not pussyfooting around in the shadows, but what works even better is to cease searching for *any* substitute word. Simply approach every event as something you are either going to *do* or *not do* and quit driving yourself crazy by hassling over things you have no real intention of doing. Your ground of being then becomes a commitment, rather than a cop-out.

When you get rid of "try" you will rid yourself of the concept of failure. It works!

Now that we have fully examined the word "try," I will give you a few more which you may measure at your leisure, using the yardstick we've been using: *Maybe, Wish* and *Hope*. Dump them! They're about as positive as the Tooth Fairy!

Chapter 4

Hypnosis / Alpha State

I would like to stress that we are all subject to natural laws that are binding upon us. The cycle I am about to offer you is called the natural cycle and it governs not only hypnosis, but everything you do. It is as much fact as, "Any idea you hold to be true is binding upon you."

You do not have to activate this cycle, it is instilled within you. It is a part of your living mechanism and all you can do is recognize it and use it, or ignore it and suffer. Just leave it alone and it will perform beautifully, for that is the way the cycle is programmed.

The beginning is simply relaxation. This is the source of all you seek for when you relax, your mind and body are working together. They refurbish your regenerative being, taking your body's nutrition and tensions, and converting them into good, pure energy . . . energy we store in our nervous systems, ready for use as needed. To be totally beneficial we must use this energy in specific ways. It cannot just be frittered away without plan, but must be used as nature designed it, through *directed activity*.

Let's define directed activity by looking at the antithesis. *Non*-directed activity breaks the cycle. Non-directed activity is the source of nail-biting, pacing the floor, twisting a lock of hair or tapping the foot impatiently. Go to a maternity ward and watch the expectant fathers. What an unrelaxed bunch they are. They break the cycle, clearly.

Directed activity completes the cycle. You expend the energy, physical or emotional, then you rest, relax, restore your energy level, and expend it once again. It is how we live and how we function . . . a natural cycle.

Whereas non-directed activity is, in effect, a product of inner conflict, directed activity has an outlet . . . it seeks a purpose. Non-directed activity is done to compensate for something else. Our mind tells us we are nervous so we bite our nails . . . a non-directed or goal-less use of energy. Smoking is a non-directed activity.

For contrast, look at the long-distance swimmer. He strokes and momentarily rests between strokes. Relaxation is a scheduled part of his training. Everything we do depends upon this cycle.

Be certain you get this important point. This natural cycle must be allowed to function. When you break the cycle of spend-restore, spend-restore, you end up smoking, nail-biting, foot-tapping and hair-twisting. You can easily restore the expended energy by alpha training, by self-hypnosis.

Hypnosis or the alpha state is based upon total relaxation, and as you practice, you increase the strength of your relaxation. The more relaxed the state you reach, the more energy you restore and the more activities you find yourself able to accommodate.

People who practice alpha training naturally become more creative, active, aware and spontaneous. Remember, it is these people who shunt their conscious mind aside and truly get in tune with their subconscious, understanding and transforming it to accommodate their true being.

Incidentally, there is a seemingly paradoxical side effect to this re-charging of our batteries, in that the more energy we have, the more we slow down in one important area—observation and consideration. Let's say you're completely in tune with your being, using alpha regularly. Your friends see you as a human dynamo, yet you're driving down the street so relaxed you begin seeing things you have never noticed before. The reason is simple. Relaxed, your mind slows down and you begin to take in more of that which is around you. As you observe more, you also consider more. You feed your subconscious data bank much more information, and are able to use that new data constructively. As you gain more energy through relaxation in your cycle, you also create the ability to relax automatically when your energy is not being called upon. Like the swimmer, you stroke, then rest. You attend to business driving from 23rd to 26th street and from 26th to 40th street, you take in the neighborhood buildings and the interesting people, truly seeing them for the first time.

Now, you ask, "How about sleep? Isn't that our automatic rejuvenator?" The key word in your question is "automatic." Yes, when you sleep, the natural cycle holds true in that your conscious mind does automatically rest, however, we have two "minds" to take care of, do we not? Here's what happens in sleep:

The conscious mind powers the outer shell, the large muscles, our voluntary machinery. The subconscious mind powers the inner core, all the visceral organs, the sense fibers and nerves . . . everything inside that functions without your conscious assistance.

Now, the natural cycle: you go to sleep, the conscious mind goes out to lunch, in effect becoming *un*conscious. When this happens the outer shell relaxes and grows limp. There you have the completed cycle for your conscious mind. It has obeyed every command all day, lifting, walking, talking, judging, deciding, and now you give it some rest... you re-charge the batteries. Energy is being restored and made ready to supply your body all the moves and processes your conscious mind will demand of it upon awakening.

Not so, the subconscious mind. Remember, the subconscious never rests, never goes to sleep, never relaxes on its own . . . instead, it retains the tensions in the inner core. So, picture this:

You are sound asleep, your outer shell or voluntary muscles and thinking processes are relaxed, re-charging, but your inner core is still functioning, handling, receiving, processing, growing tighter and tighter. The subconscious mind was never told to relax, and remember it lacks the ability to assume it should. It can only receive, date-stamp, file and feel. When you go to bed worried, upset, uptight, the last thing you think about remains with you through the night at the subconscious level, so your inner core gets more and more steel-tense.

In this process, as it functions, the subconscious continues converting energy, but now its source of energy is limited. The conscious mind, now asleep, can't supply the subconscious with data. In order to keep this inner core firm, to keep on with its job of converting, it syphons off energy from the outer shell. In other words, while your outer shell is building up energy for the day ahead, the subconscious is robbing it of the new reserves.

Imagine your car in the garage with a battery charger

hooked up all night. In the morning the battery is fully charged, since there was no drain during charging. Now repeat the process only this time leave your lights and the air-conditioner on. How much fresh power will you have come morning? The same thing happens while you sleep if you do not instruct your subconscious mind to relax.

Among your friends you can probably think of some who seem to sleep all the time, ten, twelve hours a night and yet, they never seem rested. Usually they are quick to become ill-tempered and the first to indicate a lack of energy. The reason is simple; the inner core is hard as a rock and is draining off their energy while they sleep. Their natural cycle is broken. This is why people have heart attacks, ulcers, hardening of the arteries and other physical manifestations of a mind under stress and tension. All these infirmities are directly linked to years and years of tensions stored in the visceral organs.

We know that most heart attacks are the direct result of worry and tension, but it doesn't mean we cannot absorb our share of such emotions and still function. We do, however, need the regular rest periods, the re-charging periods. When we deny our organs these rest-breaks, they must occupy themselves with stress and worry 24 hours a day, and they break down, literally come apart!

Remember, you are the physical expression of what is in your subconscious mind. In the alpha state you teach the subconscious to relax, to loosen up that hard inner core. For some of you who have tremendous amounts of tension built up in your inner core, you'll notice a kind of drugged feeling resulting from your first few adventures into alpha. This is nothing more than that inner tension area letting go, and it is something new for you. Eventually you will develop the ability to relax the conscious and subconscious simultaneously and you will awaken totally relaxed and energized.

Whenever I stress tension as the cause of heart attacks and hardening of the arteries, I am usually challenged by diet-conscious people who insist that what you eat is equally important in maintaining a healthy heart and circulatory system. Many food faddists sincerely believe our diet is the sole control mechanism.

Let's look at some interesting facts: Let's accept we have a fantastic chemical plant in our body and what we do to that machinery is always reflected in how we feel and function. There are people in the Orient who subsist on what we would call an unbalanced, miserable diet. Some on a diet of brown rice, some on sweet potatoes ... horribly one-sided. In times of famine they consume mud to satisfy their aching stomachs and yet, do you know that Chinese doctors, in order to study heart disease have to leave their country? There's no heart disease in China to study! They have to come to this country, and boy do we have heart trouble!

Worry and its product of tension are functions of the advanced, technical nations. The agrarian nations are at the bottom of the stress-related illness scale. You rarely find a South Pacific island native with an ulcer. Some experts in our human conditioning even equate tension-related illnesses and emotional malfunctioning with the number of television sets in a given country, and I'm the last person in the world to argue with that yardstick. TV is a potent and potentially lethal influence on mankind, simply because it automatically focuses on our alpha state, our subconscious mind. Television is an extremely efficient and forceful means of programming people who do not know how to protect their subconscious state.

We covered earlier the fact that some 90% of what enters a doctor's office is psychosomatic in nature. Now, not everyone is a hypochondriac, but their mind is running things and they appear to be. Let's say a woman has just had a divorce, begins feeling lethargic, missing her periods, and tells the doctor she needs a "pill." It isn't the pill she needs, since it only treats the symptom, not the cause. What she really needs is to get in touch with her anger, frustration, pain and resentment . . . re-program her subconscious so it won't throw the problem into her physical being.

Most of what people suffer is a direct result of the ideas they feed upon, not the food. People on killer diets, 310 calories a day, can gain weight . . . any idea you hold as true is binding upon you . . . and if you believe that cauliflower or parsley will give you energy, they will do just that!

I am not out to get the medical profession on my back, but I do have one requirement for any physician who treats my own body. He must be totally dedicated to the fact that *I* want to get well. I don't want a physician who pussyfoots around, prescribing sugar pills and telling me, "Well Jim, you're just going to have to live with this condition!" The hell I will! I'll go find a doctor who will kick my rear end or knock me on the head until I am totally dedicated to getting well. You see, we hold the medical profession in such reverence and awe that we imbue within the white coated figure a power he neither deserves nor in most instances wishes to have. With this kind of idol-worship going for him, when he says, "Well, you're just going to have to suffer with this," our subconscious says, "Hey, he's right! After all, he's the doctor!" I don't want my mind saying, "Yes Boss," to that kind of negative input!

No, I am not anti-doctor or anti-medicine. I know that some doctors do indeed deal with placebos, prescribing dextrose pills when there is no discernable, physiological reason for the patient's complaint. Since they do not have time to become the patient's psychologist, psychiatrist and hypnotist to find what the "problem" really is, they prescribe the sugar pill and state with confidence that three days later, the ills will be gone. They use their idol role for a positive result, and three days later, the patient calls and thanks his physician for curing his "illness."

The human mind can discount any chemical, if programmed properly. Give a hypnotized subject a water-glass full of booze and tell him it is a diet cola and he won't get drunk. Give him a glass of diet cola and tell him it is straight Jim Beam and he won't be able to stand up! I have had parties at my own home and have served the world's finest martini right out of my cold-water tap!

In my own experience I am not licensed to practice medicine nor do I wish to be. Before I became a professional there was a time in my past when friends would sometimes ask for advice. On one such occasion a friend, whose wife was far past her nine month delivery date, was so distressed he was reduced to skin and bones. Finally, his wife had the baby, and despite his tremendous relief he still could not sleep. He was so tired he looked terrible! "I know you have something that will help me," he said. Well, that was the clue. He *knew* I had just what he needed to make him sleep. "I've just got to get some sleep," he said, "I've got to sleep!"

In this case, I was the guru, the healer, the physician, and I decided to accept the appointed role. I said, "Okay, but look, keep your mouth shut! I've got some pills that are prescription . . . they're brand new . . . and if my doctor found out..."

I went out to my car and from a box of Good and Plenty candies, I selected a pink one and a white one. I put them into an envelope and gave them to him.

"Be very careful," I told him, "these are extremely potent. They are very expensive. The pink one has an 8-hour timer built into it and the white one has no timer at all." I concluded with, "These are very strong. I would suggest you do not bite into them, just take them with water or they will taste terrible. I want you to be in bed when you take the pill, since they are extremely fast acting. Swallow it and out you go!"

Well, naturally, he went home, took the pink one, had the best sleep of his life, and saved the white one for his wife when she got home from the hospital.

All this relates to more than just medicine, because—*any idea you hold to be true is binding upon you.*

Thanks to Bela Lugosi, and other Hollywood "villains," an air of mystery and witchcraft has become associated with hypnosis. Mention the subject to some people and they conjure up visions of black coated sorcerers performing mysterious primitive rites while forcing vestal virgins to submit against their will to some villainous warlock's perverted bidding. (Just as an exercise, what did *your* mind associate with "hypnosis" as you read the last sentence?)

Self-hypnosis is not witchcraft. There is nothing mysterious about bringing on the same state of mind you pass through inadvertently a dozen times a day. It is not only as easy as relaxing, it *is* relaxing. The conscious mind is in charge of the outer shell, the voluntary body functions. When you want to get in touch with the subconscious, you quiet the outer shell . . . the physical body. You relax and thus enter the "mysterious" alpha state . . . just like you do when you're driving or watching TV or a sunset. Later on I will give you a simple process for reaching the alpha state. Once the conscious mind is drowsy and pushed aside, we can contact the subconscious without being attacked. The monitoring system that directs the impulses from the body to the mind now goes into disuse—there are no impulses originating in the body to stimulate the conscious mind. The body is quiet, the mind is quiet, the subconscious comes to the fore and becomes extremely receptive.

As beginners, I urge students to do nothing but practice this relaxation technique. It is not necessary to tell yourself anything yet . . . just practice getting into and out of alpha. You will soon become familiar with the feeling of it and it will become natural. If you begin to analyze it, think about it, you activate your conscious mind, and the alpha state fades, retarding your progress. It's a matter of concentrating solely on absolutely nothing. I know that may sound puzzling, but it is easily done with practice and you develop the *feel* or the sense of the self-hypnosis state . . . the alpha state.

Eventually, with the processes you learn in the Alpha Workshop, you set up the signals for entering the alpha state as simply as you learn to drive a car. You don't question and analyze whenever you get behind the wheel or shift gears . . . it is an automatic memory reaction which does the job. You enter alpha in the same manner—with practice.

Some of what I teach to students comes from what I learn from them. I get feedback which enables me to use seminar graduates as a kind of elite group, and I learn from their successes and their failures. I'd like to share one important finding which came from this source:

Some of you who confine your alpha-state practicing to the time just before your natural evening's sleep may find yourself dropping off into a sound sleep midway in your process. Remember that you are completely relaxing your outer shell, the physical being, and once so relaxed, the desire for sleep is a natural consequence. I suggest you use your alpha-state powers at other times of the day as well. If you do it solely as a pre-sleep exercise your mind will get natural sleep (Theta) and self-hypnosis (Alpha) so intermingled, you will simply doze off. The subconscious mind learns rapidly and will automatically assume it is your desire to sleep, so it's, "Yes Boss," and sleep you will! There's nothing wrong with using alpha to get a restful, natural sleep, but if your purpose is to re-organize your data bank you're robbed of the opportunity.

Chapter 5

The Conning Tower

"Con: To swindle a victim by first gaining his *con*-fidence. To trick or fool by glib persuasion."

We all have our own "conning tower," and like the submarine, ours is also below the surface. It is our excuse for our cop-outs. The dictionary defines cop-out as an act of confessing (usually of a guilt or inadequacy) . . . the act of reneging or quitting.

I really enjoy this "Conning Tower" analogy. A conning tower is a control position, usually submerged and used by means of a very narrow field of vision which we must sweep 360-degrees to understand our surroundings. To me, that sounds like an adequate description of our own control position—our mind.

The vehicles we use to con ourselves are the same—visual images and the words that befit them. Although we have already devoted a chapter to the words we use, let's add a few more—the ones we most often use in our "conning tower."

Ever had a problem? Yes? What you had in fact was a situation which required additional thought or energy. "Problem" belongs right up there with "T-R-Y." Just how did contemporary man get so caught up in "problems"? Freudian psychiatrists will scream bloody murder, but I have to name old Sigmund as the founder of "problems."

When Sigmund Freud finally gained acceptance in the early 1920's he toured the United States, lecturing on his theory of psychoanalysis. This was a period in U.S. history fraught with the uncertainty of a rising stock market and too much money. Since Freudian psychiatry focused on what was "wrong," an entire nation became obsessed with its "problems." It was new, it was popular and it appeared to answer the need at that time for clarity amid confusion. People began to have "problems" just so they could join their peers in psychoanalysis. The fields of analysis, psychology, hypnotism became problem oriented. If you think there is a plethora of published material on the subject of human awareness today, you should have seen the flood of data prevalent in the 20's!

Over that generation, 1920 to about 1931, this conception of problem awareness was hammered into the nation's combined minds. The field of analytical psychiatry really got off the ground, but it was unfortunately problem oriented. This is why we today use the term mental "illness," i.e. a sickness, i.e. a problem, i.e. "wrong!"

Believe me, focusing on a problem only adds to the problem itself. Let me show you this simple diagram:

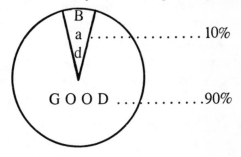

Imagine this: you are the 100% circle. 10% of you consists of the negative garbage of your life. Here is where you have stored the Greek grandmother, her wine and garlic, your aversion to spinach and elevators, what-have-you.

The remaining 90% of your being is your magnificence, your beauty and human goodness. This is the area in which you truly play.

One of the laws of nature is that for something to grow, it must in some way be nurtured. If you have a weed a few feet from a lovely rose bush, but you water and tend only the weed, what will happen to your roses? The weed will flourish and spread its seeds all over the county as the roots of the rose bush atrophy and die.

When you focus attention on your 10% area, even if only through a weekly visit to your friendly psychiatrist, you continually nurture the "bad." You thus dwell on *why* the bad, *how* the bad, *when* the bad, etc. Gradually your "good" atrophies and will eventualiy die or certainly malfunction. When you continually concentrate and "worry" about your "problems" you reaffirm their very existence! You actually support their occupation of that 10% of your being!

When you use the word "problem" you are emphasizing an obstacle and generating a feeling of helplessness—concentrating on the obstacle before you rather than striving for the solution. Please get this: *Problems exist solely in the mind of the beholder.*

Ready for another analogy? Okay, are you as intelligent as a squirrel? Watch a squirrel and you will note he spends considerable time collecting a cache of nuts and goodies which he stores in his tree-home. What happens when lightning strikes the tree and it crashes to the ground? In an instant, his home is gone, his food supply burned. He literally has nothing! Does he run around moaning over his misfortune? Does he start bad-rapping the forest and mother nature for his plight or go lay down on some wise old owl's couch to have his "problem" analyzed? No, he just finds another tree, builds another nest and sets about gathering another cache of nuts. Do you know why? Because, dammit, *that's his job!*

Please eliminate that word "problem." When you discuss something you are dealing with, use a word that fits the circumstances, the difficulty, the challenge. In fact, use the word "challenge" because it is purpose oriented . . . a positive and not a negative. Once again you become acutely aware that it's *how you hold it!*

Okay, here's another cop-out word we transmit from our conning tower: *it!* Here's how we abdicate our responsibility and get into the "let George do it" syndrome. Someone says, "Every time I get up in front of an audience, *it* happens." How about, "I can't help *it?*" What you're saying is you cannot help *yourself.* The subconscious tosses up the word "it" as something outside your responsibility.

When you begin saying "myself" in this context, instead of "it," you immediately begin to assume your responsibility. Since we hesitate to admit we can't help ourselves in a situation, we phase out that tiny but powerful "it."

When overweight people say, "Whenever I pass the refrigerator, *it* comes over me," they're asking us to believe the word "it" is sitting on top of the refrigerator pulling them toward the goodies inside. "It" doesn't open the door and cram the cheesecake down their throat, they do that.

I'll give you two more words with connected dangers: "I have." Remember that anything you hold to be true is binding upon you, and when you say, "I have this problem," then congratulations, you have just married that problem. "I have" should be used only for positive thought. It's a powerful connective between what you *think* and what you *believe*. It may sound like stretching a point, but the person who goes around saying, "I have a cold," will suffer more and longer than one who says, "I am recovering from a cold."

Remember your subconscious is your obedient, "Yes Boss" servant. When you say, "I have this drinking problem" or "I have a horrible cold" your mind simply agrees with you. Don't feed your mind negative garbage! Feed it positive thought!

Before you set about to dismantle your own conning tower, to remove that source of negativity, let me give you a better idea. All you need do is alter how you use it. Use it to "con" yourself in a positive direction.

Remember what we have learned about reprogramming our subconscious? Okay, when you encounter a situation which is a difficult challenge, instead of saying the old "I have a problem," you can "con" your mind into coughing up the solution by saying, "I have the ability to solve the situation." Somewhere in your data bank of past experiences is the answer and your mind-servant will say, "Yes Boss," and serve it up to you!

Now I'll give you the two most powerful words in the English language which fit this context. They are, *I AM!* These are the words which can take something and make it a part of you. Your obedient subconscious mind waits eagerly for these two words, because what immediately follows them is its firm directive. What follows the *I am* becomes *you*. This is why I urge my students to display that sign: *"Never say you are anything you do not wish to be!"*

Used negatively, *I am* becomes downright vicious. I am tired. I am helpless. I am sick. You immediately weld what follows to your being and you are then indeed tired, helpless or sick!

Rather than con yourself into a negative personality or behavior pattern by insisting, *"I have* a problem," and "I can't help *it,"* and *"I am* helpless," just change how you hold it. Become a person who says, *"I have* the solution, I can help *myself* and *I am* powerful."

Feed your mind the positive word-food it needs to feed back to you in your thoughts and attitudes, and your life will become full and rewarding. You are the unconscious architect of your own circumstances and you can become fully aware of that.

Chapter 6

The Rules of the Mind

Good rules serve good purposes. Our lives are full of rules and they begin as soon as our conscious mind begins operating. An eighty-year old person will still look both directions before crossing a street. Early in life we are given the Golden Rule, which I prefer to paraphrase as: "Do unto yourself as you would have others do unto you." It is our rules which keep ships in the harbor from colliding and motorists from driving on the wrong side of the road.

When we strive to function without rules we end in small and large disasters. Unfortunately we are flooded with rules throughout our entire life and often become so inundated with these directives we tend to ignore them. When you bring home your new hi-fi stereo set and open the carton, there on top is the owner's manual. These are the rules for reaping the full benefits of your marvelous new music system, and yet, how many times do we toss the manual aside and start hooking up the wires? Fortunately for us the engineers have designed into the unit some secondary and tertiary safety systems, almost as though they knew our mind would step in and disregard the rules.

When the hi-fi fails to work and we reluctantly pick up the manual as a last resort, we're lucky the whole system hasn't gone "blooey!"

It is only natural that something as profound and powerful and influencing on your life as the subconscious must surely have specifications for you to follow, and I would like to list them for you. There are seven rules of the mind and they govern its functioning. (In our Alpha Workshop seminars we dwell strongly on each of them, however, for our purposes here we will examine four of the most cogent.)

The more you understand these rules the more you will gain self-appreciation; using your mind as it was designed to be used.

1. EVERY THOUGHT OR IDEA CAUSES A PHYSICAL REACTION.

We have discussed the nightmare of falling and the physiological consequences of this "thought." We have mentioned the "endorphins," the body's own opiate which our mind creates when we believe we are receiving a pain-killer. I have shown you how thinking "sand" and "desert" creates thirst. This phenomenon is the basis for our natural law that everything we hold to be true is binding upon us.

Remember we cannot separate the body from the mind. The subconscious mind is the brain *and* the nervous system and it affects not most of our body, but all of it. That which affects the mind affects the body, it's as simple as that.

The stronger the idea, the stronger the physical impact. Recall the process? An idea enters our conscious mind which passes along the formed image to our subconscious which then returns it to us as an attitude. This is physical repetition, and each thought and each idea does create a physical response. In fact a science has evolved from this phenomenon called kinetics, or dynamics. It is the branch of mechanics dealing with the motions of material bodies under the action of given forces.

Remember this first rule of the mind—every thought or idea causes a physical reaction. When you hear something exciting you get goose-bumps. When you observe a sad movie sequence your throat tightens and tears flow. Your entire being-world consists of ideas and feelings. If you do not have the feeling you wish and you know that ideas cause physical responses fed by the subconscious, then just load up that 88% of your brain with whatever it is you desire. Don't dwell on what you don't want, just remember the power of "I am" and put it to work for you.

You *can* alter your whole outward physical disposition by just changing your thinking. This is infallible. It will always work and there are no exceptions!

2. WHAT IS EXPECTED TENDS TO BE REALIZED.

Basically, your expectations and anticipations are the promises you make to yourself—promises you are going to have to keep. Whether constructive or destructive, these expectations will tend to be realized. The brain and nervous system respond to mental images, regardless of their source. Your idea or thought becomes a blueprint for the subconscious mind to use in building a goal. One of the fantastic facets of your mind is its goal-seeking capability. Remember it delights in saying "Yes Boss," and then doing its job. If you expect to do well, you will then do well. If you expect to do poorly, you program yourself accordingly.

Earlier I told you that worry was simply an act of

concentrating on what it is you do *not* want. When you build the image of what is unwanted, your subconscious cannot differentiate between what has been and what is to be, it can only head for that "goal."

At the Psychonetix Centre in Tarzana we conduct Money Seminars, designed to focus a new awareness on our attitudes toward money, wealth and poverty. What most people are amazed to discover is that their lack of financial success can be traced back to early subconscious input.

Let's take the case of a child who grows up with constant reminders that his family is poor. All he ever hears is, "We can't afford it. Money is scarce. We have to save or we'll all starve." When he rubs his nose against a candy counter window he hears the same old story. He wants a bicycle like other kids on the block and gets fed the same data. Over a period of time he is so conditioned to poverty it becomes his way of life ... the way he holds money and wealth. At age 40 he is still bemoaning his financial failure, still cannot afford "it" and still has no money. He will not stick his neck out for that job advancement because it's an unknown, even though what he *does* know pays less and is less rewarding. He settles for what he has because to venture out of that low paying but secure space is totally against his upbringing. The subconscious, so programmed, keeps him poor.

Oddly enough it is such people who, when faced with winning the Irish Sweepstakes or receiving a substantial inheritance, will soon go through their windfall and re-establish the original state of poverty. It is all the subconscious will allow them to know. Here's another example:

On her first day in kindergarten Sally is befriended by Johnny, the first real friend she has ever had. She has come to associate love with good feelings toward others, so she "loves" Johnny. A few months later Johnny's family moves to another state and Sally is heartbroken.

Sally has two other puppy-love experiences in elementary school and both boys transfer out of the district, again accenting the love/loss pattern.

In high school, having suffered from love-associations, Sally is more reserved, aloof from the boys in her class, but Harvey befriends her and begins carrying her books home. Although Harvey does his best to break through Sally's protective barrier, he cannot bring her out of her own reservations, and he finally gives up and drops her.

The association between liking, feeling affection and loving, and being hurt, is now firmly planted in Sally's mind. Chances are excellent that Sally will never get married and settle for "Aunt Sally" the rest of her life.

Loving and losing was what she had come to *expect*, and that is exactly what she got.

Remember, what you expect you will realize. When you practice your alpha training expect the very best from it and you will get it. Never expect less than the very best of yourself and old "Yes Boss" will deliver for you, happily. That's its job!

3. IMAGINATION IS MORE POWERFUL THAN KNOWLEDGE OR REASON. REASON IS EASILY OVERRULED BY IMAGINATION.

This can be proven at the outset by pure mathematics: 88 over 12. Your 88% mind easily dominates the other 12%. Anytime you pit reason (the conscious mind) against imagination (the subconscious), the subconscious mind will win hands down. Your imagination is the strongest weapon in your arsenal and nothing in your psychic make-up can defend against it. (Unfortunately this holds true for the bad as well as the good.)

Let's say that vacation trip to Europe is completely out of the question for you. You lack the funds, the time off from work, even the knowledge of how in the world you would go about planning such an event. All you need do is get into your alpha state . . . shunt aside your argumentative conscious mind . . . and use your imagination. Picture yourself at the airport, waving to friends as you depart . . . touring the Tower of London and the Vatican . . . dining by candlelight in Paris. Go for it! Then "wake up" and go about your business, but every day repeat the process.

When you feed this imagined trip into the subconscious, it again can only say, "Yes Boss" and surprisingly, events in your life begin to lead in the desired direction, toward your European vacation. Without realizing it you may tune in on a conversation which opens up a new job opportunity with an airline. Mr. Wonderful comes into your life and since he is financially able, he offers such a trip. Funny things will begin to happen; ideas, urges, inspirations, and before you realize it, you're at the airport waving goodbye to friends!

I said earlier that this power of your imagination holds true for the bad as well as the good. Let's examine a negative example:

Assume your company or organization is sending you to an important convention, and as their representative they have committed you to address the gathering on the procedures or successes your group has effected. Let's say that public speaking was your least favorite subject in school and every time you spoke before large audiences a lot of past traumas surfaced. Even though that was twenty years ago, you still suffer those fears. Can you hear yourself discussing the upcoming convention with your spouse?

"Good grief, what will I say? I can just *imagine* myself getting up there on the stage and making a complete ass of myself! *Imagine* how embarrassed I'll be?"

Okay, guess who's going to stand up there and be a complete ass? Guess who's going to be embarrassed? That's the way you have it wired, and that's the way your subconscious will serve it up to you! "Yes Boss!"

Accept this fact: Your imagination is the greatest tool you have. Train it! Use it! It will bring *anything* your way, desirable or undesirable, it doesn't make any difference. It will bring you bitterness, unhappiness or failure. It will bring you friends, fame, fortune and love. It's up to you!

4. ONLY ONE IDEA CAN BE ENTERTAINED AT ANY GIVEN TIME: TWO OPPOSING IDEAS CANNOT BE ENTERTAINED BY THE MIND SIMULTANEOUSLY.

Let me refer you back to the 100% circle of your being; the 10% "bad" and the 90% "good." We talked then about the "nurturing" of one or the other of those two segments. Rule four simply states that you cannot nurture both at the same time.

Freudian psychoanalysis says you have to concentrate on the "bad," find out *why* the "bad," *how* the "bad," *when* the "bad," etc. When you're all through with your analysis you're worse off than before because all you've been talking about, i.e. nurturing, is the "bad."

All you need do is identify the "bad," know it's there and then, with alpha training, begin processing the subconscious with "good." Dwell on "good," feed it, nurture it, accent it, make it grow!

You are planting the direct opposite of "bad" firmly in the subconscious, focusing all your energies on all that is good. Since both bad and good are like two plants springing from the same soil, when you feed one it is always at the expense of the other. Keep feeding the "good" no matter how much "bad" screams and yells. Soon "bad" will shrivel as "good" grows. You cannot feed one without robbing the other. Recognize the ability you truly possess for transforming the subconscious and—do your job.

Chapter 7

The End of Puppeteering

In early English history one of the most popular touring attractions was the puppet show. The puppeteers would roll through the countryside with their miniature theatres, their puppet characters dancing to unseen hands at the end of many strings. More often than not, the theme of these mini-plays dealt with the struggle of the poorer class against the power vested in royalty and land owners. These plots were the delight of the common folk and had analysis been popular in that time I would venture to say this popularity would have been recognized as purely vicarious. It was an escape, through humor, from their own miserable state of serfdom.

Oddly enough, puppeteering is widely popular today, only we do it with real people! We pull other people's strings, or more commonly, we push their buttons, to compensate for our own "miserable state."

Strings, buttons or reins, no matter what we call them, they become our manipulators. Let's use "reins" for another analogy.

When you're born, all the reins are inherent within

you. You have a built-in autonomy of being; however, very early in our lives we begin giving them away. We relinquish one to our mother, one to our father, we give the teacher one of our reins and one to the kid down the block who threatens to beat us up. As we grow, we forfeit a rein to the mate we want to win and the boss we want to please.

Imagine yourself starting out driving an eight horse stage coach team, each horse with two reins. All sixteen reins are securely in hand and the horses answer your bidding with the slightest tug. Now begin handing them out as you travel along life's road until fourteen are held by others, and you control but two. *Now* attempt to handle all that horsepower by yourself. You can't do it, not without manipulating other people in an effort to gain their assistance.

In behavior science an experiment was made with a spider spinning a web. The spider was given a disorienting drug and he went crazy! Where his normal web-spinning pattern was uniform and structurally sound, he ended up with a maze of senseless threads, randomly connected with no plan or structural integrity. He didn't control his "strings."

Okay, let's call these control mechanisms, "buttons." Kids are the most beautiful button pushers of all. Give a youngster an insight into one of your weaknesses and watch him go to work! He visits grandma and when refused something he says, "When I'm home, mom lets me do it!" Whenever a child wants attention, he knows full well which button to push on whom.

Now I want you to get this next point: People who go around pushing buttons, pulling strings or reins are not doing it because they're stronger than others. The exact opposite is true. A weak individual who has no character of his own, who is nothing but a collection of fears, anxiety, guilt and "insecurity"—rather than admit to this and express it honestly—will run around pulling everyone else's strings. He enjoys a perverse pleasure in setting people up. He becomes keenly observant of his fellow man and can walk into a room, select his victim, and in one or two choice words, send his victim straight up the wall. These are the people who elbow their way through life, giving the appearance of being aggressive, forceful, secure, but the reverse is true. They are scared to death!

The old cliché that "life is short" is a pure truism. If you were to live your maximum of 200 years, it would still be too short. It's certainly too short to become anyone's puppet. It's too precious to give out even one rein to another person. To live life fully you must decide your own destiny . . . live your own life . . . not at the expense of others, but with a total responsibility *for* yourself and *to* your fellow man.

Now then, what facet of a person's character could possibly turn them into a button pusher or puppeteer? It is the same emotional trait that stands between you and everything in this world you desire—*resistance!* Log this as another fact of life. Now, let's examine the connotation of the word:

Resistance is any idea, thought, attitude or feeling which is negative. When I learned this it was as though the sky had opened to allow the sun to shine for the very first time! It was only when I learned this that I began to plot my own course through life. Let me explain:

You cannot take an objective view of your own life. It's impossible because you are the center of your own life and thus, all that you survey is the result of your own thinking. Your thinking and your emotions produce your attitudes and they color every single thing you perceive. What one person perceives is not always what another sees. Where you may see opportunity and success, another may see only fear and failure.

Since you are inescapably and intrinsically involved in yourself, you cannot abandon your own ship. When you put out resistance, it will always return to you and you wind up actually resisting yourself. Anytime you express a negative idea, a negative thought or attitude or feeling, it's like tossing out a boomerang or a homing pigeon. Ever attempt to throw away a homing pigeon? This may seem difficult to accept, but let's examine it:

First, let's apply a rule: *Negating any idea only makes it stronger.* Someone says to you, "I think you are a bad person. You hurt other people." Your first reaction is to defend yourself by saying, "I am *not*. I do *not!*" The *not* is your clue ... it means you are resisting. "Not" is by definition and connotation a negative. "Not" does not stand on its own two feet any more than "try." Both words need amplification. When you say, "I am not," the counter is, "you are not *what?*"

Remember we said our subconscious mind sits ready to pounce on your thoughts, but it can't compute "not," so it latches on to what immediately follows. When you say, "I am not tired," you are welding that powerful "I am" with the emotion or feeling which follows. "Tired" is the feeling, rather than the nebulous "not." You only reinforce the "tired" and make the thing you *don't* want even stronger. "Tired" becomes the homing pigeon you wish to throw away. What you really meant was, "I am energetic!"

There is no more frustrating experience in life than having to defend an untruth, yet people rise to the chal-

lenge with their defensive, "I am *not!*" If you are called a
liar, resisting "liar" makes it stronger. The subconscious
picks it up and you find yourself not only acting like one,
but feeling like one!

Let's suppose a man is accused of stealing, although
he is in fact innocent. "You stole," says the officer. "I did
not steal," comes the reply. He continually responds with
"I did not steal, I did not steal." By the time he comes
before the judge to prove his innocence he has taken on the
attitude of a person who steals. He acts *guilty,* as though he
had something to hide. He has psychically interpreted
everything he does in the light of the untruth.

You do not have to accept any thought or idea that
comes to you, regardless the source. Rather than rise to
your own defense (I am *not!*) recognize the other person's
right to think and do as he pleases. This doesn't mean you
go through life as somebody's doormat. Here's an example:

A man raises his hand and says to me, "I think you're
a quack!" My reply is, "All right, I recognize your right to
think anything you choose, but be careful that what you
believe is based upon truth and not fear." Has he made me
look bad? I have not sprung to my defense by replying, "I
am *not* a quack!" Were I to do that I would be on the
defensive and I would thus diminish my own being, de-
mean myself. *Always* reply to a negative accusation with a
simple truth and you gain by the experience. It changes a
dispute into a simple exchange of opinion. Debates which
lead to heated arguments are the triggers which release all
the old, pent-up garbage of our past experiences and since
the mind cannot deal with and dismiss the energy it
creates, it turns that energy inward, into the physical
being. The result is stress and its product of high blood

pressure, nervousness, spastic colons and heart attacks.

Let me give you an analogy which clearly shows how resentment starts its chain-reaction. There are four steps to incapacitation which I call the "Blueprint for Self Destruction."

I have already offered a few examples of things in our life that are absolutely, totally and without exception, truisms. I'd like to share one with you now that transcends the theoretical, one that is an unarguable part of our human engineering . . . the way we are constructed and designed to function. You don't get to vote on this one. If you don't like it, then that's tough because you don't have a choice when it comes to a fact. It is a state of being most people refuse to take seriously and once they understand its power, admit to years of needless suffering. It's called: *Passivity.*

Bear in mind that you are an electro-static, bio-chemical, psycho-dynamic, self contained unit. You operate on electrical energy . . . you have constant chemical changes to contend with . . . you have inertial guidance systems functioning within your mind . . . and you are not using anyone else's power source. You are indeed self contained. Now then, the energy you constantly generate *must be dealt with*. Follow this example:

You are in a room and someone yells, "fire!" You immediately generate the energy to remove yourself from the room. The door is opened, you and the others rush out to a safe distance, and you stop. You have expended the energy you created to conclude the intended goal. You have dealt with it.

Now let's alter the scene a bit. Someone yells, "fire" and the crowd rushes out, slamming the door in your face. It is locked from the outside, trapping you in the potentially deadly room. Are you relaxed? No, you are a container of excess energy with no place to empty it. Your sole purpose in life is to get out of that room. You don't care about your teeth and gums and fingernails, and if it comes right down to it, you will chew and scratch right through the door panel. You don't care if you get hurt or whether the room is on the first or fifteenth floor. You can go into almost total panic. Does the energy subside, or does it build? It builds, and builds, until you can actually go totally, hysterically insane. That is the energy I am talking about. Right now, as you read this in your relaxed state, were I to activate your brain and prevent you from releasing the energy you create, you would go bananas. In the first "fire" instance, you dealt with it, and in the second, you did not . . . so:

Step number one: In order to start the chain reaction, something happens in your life. It can be anything; a telephone ringing, a horn or doorbell, a death in the family, anything . . . but you do nothing about it. You exercise *passivity* and let it slide.

Suppose you are a lady walking happily through the shopping plaza and you note an approaching friend. Your mind recognizes her and you're going to say "hello." Let's assume it takes ten units of energy to complete your goal, so you generate the ten units. Unfortunately, your friend walks by without noticing you, continuing on into the crowd. This brings us to:

Step number two: *Over-adapting*. The very second you are denied spending your ten units of energy, releasing the energy, you over-adapt to it. You begin to make it grandiose or larger than life. Your mind speeds up and you think, "Who does she think she is?" Your mind is off and running. "After all I've done for her, the snob! She buys a new blouse and she's too good for me . . . who does she think she is . . . blah, blah, blah!'' Your mind goes crazy because those ten units of energy were not released, and as step two jumps in, something else happens: Every time you move from one step to another, the energy doubles. You now have *twenty* units of energy built up. Your mind speeds. It reaches into your circuitry, pulls out plugs and patch-cords, plugs in others, and what comes up for you are all the old insults, the past rejections and insecurities, all the unresolved "stuff" of your past.

You label your current dilemma as an "upset" but it has nothing to do with being snubbed by your friend. Upsets are always wired into something else, something from your past. Most people don't handle an upset when it happens, making it "right" or dealing with it, so they get a chance to dip back into their past hurts and work on the unfinished business. The upset remains, and simply adds itself to all the others you hold.

Steps one and two are invisible. They are inside the head. You don't get to see them because they are purely internal. It is step three which becomes visible.

Step number three: *Agitation*. Your twenty units of energy, in making the jump to step three, double again. Now you are burdened with *forty* units of unreleased energy. Your mind has built up the situation out of all proportion, your head swimming with its new and heavy load, so the mind says, "Enough, already!" The mind has other more important work to do so it dumps the built up energy into your body and the body obediently picks it up. Here is the first time you get to see all this energy as it manifests itself in the form of nail-biting, floor pacing, clicking a fountain pen, playing with a lock of hair or tapping the foot nervously. Cigarette smoking is certainly agitation, as is overeating. These are all the result of step three in our blueprint for self destruction.

This agitation, when it surfaces in the physical body, is a *symptom*. When you see these "symptoms," don't mistake them for the "problems." They are step three, remember. It means there is something that hasn't been dealt with.

Interestingly, when the mind finally releases those forty units into the body, getting rid of it, the mind slows back down. It doesn't have to deal with it any longer, the body has it . . . it's the body's problem now. Many people foolishly use hypnosis to shut off visible agitation, but that amounts only to symptom removal. It is one reason why the medical profession looks so unkindly upon hypnotists. Stop-smoking clinics and weight-reduction clinics encounter difficulty in this area since all they do is shut off the smoking, the overeating, when they are only the *symptoms*. They represent only the physical manifestations of step number one! The "problem" still exists! Ever notice when you quit smoking how you begin barking at people, crabbing at the wife and shouting at the kids? You still have your "problem." All you've done is dealt with the symptom. You are now geared for unreasoning behavior, which is:

Step number four: *Incapacitation*.

Remember with each step our energy doubles, so now we are burdened with *eighty* units, and that is a heavy load. Incapacitation is also sometimes called *violence*. Here is where your mind stops. Lying in a hospital, comatose, your body full of tubes, your mind isn't bothering you one bit. It has won the battle *and* the war. Every murder evolves from these four steps. Every suicide, every case of ulcers, every cold, even every divorce, if the marriage produced passivity.

This is the four-step blueprint for incapacitation . . . for self-destruction, and if you don't particularly like it, that doesn't change a thing.

Let's say you get a divorce, but you don't clean up the mess. You hold on to those unresolved feelings, the resentments, the angers and injuries. I can promise you will end up at step four! If you have a death in the family and do not resolve it, finish it up, deal with it, you'll wind up at step four.

That's it! I don't know of a simpler, cleaner, easier way to present this blueprint for self-destruction. When you encounter step one, DEAL WITH IT AND DISMISS IT!

Getting back to the title of this chapter, you can now see how foolish and deadly it is to let your friend in the shopping plaza *pull your strings*. When you avoid resistance your whole life will take on a new mental outlook. Remember, you are the center of your own life and cannot view it objectively. It must be viewed subjectively. You and you alone have the final say over what you do and what you do not do. No other person can push your button if you do not allow it. No other person's thinking has any effect on you which you do not allow. It is not the *actions* of others which control your strings, it is your *re*actions which you alone generate.

Reach out in your mind and regather all those reins which control your horsepower. Grasp them firmly and pull them into your own being and you will gain mastery over every aspect of your life.

Chapter 8

Love vs. Sacrifice and Need

I have told you that caution must be exercised in the words we use, and this chapter deals with three words everyone mixes up. They put them into a common pot, stir them up, and when the brew becomes distasteful, wonder what went wrong with the recipe. In discussing love we need to disassociate from the romantic notions we have inherited from Tin Pan Alley. Most song writers work with the accepted concept of "love" rather than the true meaning of the word. "Oh How I Need You," or the "Without You I'm Nothing" type of lyrics do not in any way say I love you. Love is giving *from* yourself. That kind of love comes from the abundance you generate from serving yourself. If you love yourself, you can then give love. If you don't have it, how can you give it?

Sacrifice, on the other hand, is giving *of* yourself. For an example, let's change "love" to "money."

You have accumulated $10,000 and you serve yourself by investing it in a savings account. With your reason and knowledge you have supplied yourself with the opportunity not only to preserve your wealth, but get a return on

72

it. Each year that check for $600 rolls in and you still have your original amount. So, what is your attitude toward that bonus, that $600? It is free and easy, and if your spouse wants a set of golf clubs or a new evening gown you cheerfully go out and buy the present.

The principal amount, the $10,000 may represent something totally different to you. Perhaps it represents a feeling of added security in case of emergency. Along comes hubby with his desire for new golf clubs. Now, if you must part with some of that $10,000 nest egg, it is a *sacrifice*. You now must share part of the whole, and chances are that when you do so, you're going to remind hubby that he'd damn well better appreciate it! Resentment is inherent in the act of sacrificing something. Self-sacrificing people are not loved for their trait because the price they exact is too high. When we "give" anything, love, money, whatever . . . it must be given freely and our joy and contentment should come only from the act of giving itself.

Were I to give you a gift and say, "I have spent a considerable sum on this . . . a lot of time and effort . . . and I want you to wear it or use it," how does that make you feel? Trapped! If I had to "give up" something to make it happen and then make you aware of my "sacrifice," you'll probably tell me to keep it, and rightly so.

Too many people offer sacrifice, thinking it is love. The divorce courts are full of them, as are the convalescent homes. The price you pay to someone who sacrifices for you is too dear. Unthinking parents are guilty of alienating their own children by continually pounding home such thoughts as, "After all I've done for you," and "Your father and I worked our fingers to the bone for you." This does not earn warmth and affection. It does not offer an avenue for love to flow freely. Sacrifice breeds resentment.

Love, on the other hand, is serving yourself *first*. This is not selfishness. When you fall in love, who is the first one to feel the love? You are. You generate the feeling within yourself ... you accumulate love just as you accumulated that $10,000 and now that you have an abundance of love, it is yours to share.

Love is nothing more than a sharing of the quality that you yourself create, and when you have served yourself so well—as you do when you fall in love—you are generating love, releasing the love from the spill-over of your own abundance. Your reward is the counter-love you receive.

Again, self-love is not selfishness. Self-love is real love. If you love yourself it is easy for others to recognize it and they respond to it fully. A person who truly likes people automatically becomes a likeable person. We are not talking about conceit or a "holier than thou" attitude, but a deep and comfortable knowledge which makes us secure in a positive sense of our own self-worth and human goodness. True love is an effortless process since it happens spontaneously, honestly and openly. You have an abundance of love for yourself and you elect to share that feeling with others. There is no lack in giving of your own love. You are not sacrificing or giving up anything, only sharing what you have.

One deadly word many people confuse with love is "need." Need is a product of lack. Love, remember, is a product of abundance. People who love, give ... people who need, take. If you need a new car, do you have one? If you need $50, do you have $50? Of course not. If you need understanding, do you have understanding? If you need love, do you have any?

Remember you cannot entertain two opposing ideas at the same time anymore than you can go up and down simultaneously. If you have a lacking to offer, how can you offer an abundance? This means you cannot love someone you need. You can neither need someone you love. The two just do not go together.

The only thing "need" and "love" have in common is that they are both feelings, and these are your creation, remember. Need is a feeling that generates an attitude: lack. When someone generates this feeling of lack, of need, you can almost sense their reaching out for you and hanging on. This is where the proverbial green-eyed monster comes from.

Let's examine a marriage, unfortunately not an uncommon one. Assume the wife has come from a healthy and constructive background, one filled with a sharing of familial love. She has developed a firm attitude toward her own self-worth, her self-esteem, and loves herself as the person she is. She shares that love with her husband, giving from her own abundance.

Assume the husband's background is totally different. His parents extracted "payment" for the sacrifices they made for him, the upbringing, the college education. He resents the debt he must certainly owe these sacrificing parents. He is suspicious of anyone who "gives" him anything, and his own self-love is sorely lacking or nonexistent. He has no abundance of love to draw upon, so he becomes a "taker" only. Such a relationship, based on such an uneven foundation, cannot stand the stresses of marriage. One person is giving, the other is taking. The scene is set for resentment, guilt, anxiety, you name it. One person is secure, one is suspicious and jealous, so . . . call the lawyer.

Many women challenge this "need" attitude by saying they "need" their husband to bring home the pay check . . . to dry their tears over the upsets they encounter . . . to advise them in unfamiliar areas. They do not "need" their husband in those areas . . . they only rely upon him. They rely upon him to bring home the pay check since that is their arrangement at the moment. They rely upon him to respond to their tears out of his love for them. They rely upon him to have the car serviced since they are not mechanically minded. Rely, yes. Need, no. When you need, you take, when you rely upon someone you simply give them an opportunity to love you in ways that will support you.

If you want to "need" something, then focus on the five needs we all have: air to breathe . . . food and water for nourishment . . . rest and comfort . . . adequate shelter . . . sunlight and warmth. Those you do need, and *"needs" run you!*

Remember, if you need love you are telling yourself you have none, and if you have no love where must you find it? Within yourself. You are a subjective human being, revolving around your own life, not around someone else's. You don't give your life to another, you share it with them, and if you do not have that abundance of love within yourself, how can you give love to somebody else? Add "need" to "try" and get it out of your vocabulary and while you're at it, toss out "sacrifice" as well. They're all negative in definition and connotation.

The closest approximation to love is generosity. Not the generosity you experience at Christmas because our materialistic upbringing has taught us to expect a gift in return. True generosity shows us the difference between generosity and sacrifice. A truly generous person releases the gift, gives it away and that's the end of it—do with it what you will. As in the case of the golf clubs or evening gown, the act of giving is its own reward. You cannot hurt my "feelings" by not wearing or using my gift since I gave from my own abundance. What you do with the gift is not part of my act of giving. Giving or sharing out of abundance does not produce an obligation. Sacrificing does.

If your mind is still telling you all this talk of self-worth and self-love sounds selfish, then change those terms to simple self-interest. We must all have a keen interest in our own being, it is our nature. You begin with you. You cannot shake your own center of gravity and go outside yourself. You cannot say, "Here, live my life for me." You and you alone are the center of your own tiny universe. It is your nature to be subjective so you must have a healthy self-interest. You must serve yourself first, and well, so that you will have something to offer to someone else. Selfishness is not knowing where your self-interest lies. Selfishness is an inner emptiness which you attempt to fill with "something else."

A selfish person will fixate upon possessions, but a self-interested person looks upon his possessions as a kind of bounty. What really counts is his or her own being. A person who has come to terms with this supplies himself generously.

So how does all this relate to attaining the alpha state, the state of self-hypnosis? Remember that the words we use are taken in by the conscious mind, passed on to the subconscious and returned to us as an attitude. How we hold "need," "sacrifice" and "love" are functions of our own attitudes. In alpha, we can transform those feelings from their destructive past connotations, into constructive use, making them work for us. If you now recognize that you have in the past demonstrated a "need" for something or someone, you now know where to look for a new attitude—old No. 1—yourself.

Let's say you needed money in the past. You didn't desire it, you needed it, clutching after it because you never had it. Okay, now you can simply desire it. You get into the alpha state and picture yourself with all the bills marked "paid." You see yourself with money you deserve, enjoying it, investing it, sharing it with your friends and family. You repeat this process until you automatically alter your own attitude toward money and develop a strong affluent feeling within you. As in the case of the young lady who could not possibly imagine that vacation in Europe, you will find "things" beginning to take place in your life which support and nurture this new, affluent attitude. An opportunity will arise, and since your mind is transformed into a purpose-oriented entity, you recognize the opportunity and put it to use. You have replaced an old "need" with a positive attitude which becomes a fulfilled purpose.

Any lack you see within yourself must be fulfilled by you, so let yourself have it . . . give it to yourself. It is truly an enjoyable process. When you put it into practice you will become a lifelong devotee of the process and recognize, perhaps for the first time, what an enervating waste of time it has been to look outside yourself for what you desire. More people suffer from lack of application than lack of knowledge, so it becomes important for you to reach a new level of understanding of self . . . develop what amounts to a new belief system about yourself and practice it.

Most people take the path of least resistance (and if you recall, passivity is the first step toward incapacita-

tion), so don't just sit on the couch and watch television
. . . don't refuse to apply yourself to your desires. Monitor
your own thinking and put your awareness to good use.
The person who sits poaching his brain in front of the TV is
resisting the application of steps toward his own fulfillment and growing weaker as a result of that resistance.

Watch what happens when you apply these processes
to your own life. As you treat yourself as a popular person,
you feel and become popular. Treat yourself as a loving,
giving person and others will love you and support you.
Transform your own attitudes and through the alpha state,
reinforce the positive things you desire in life. Whenever
you recognize an area you would be better off without,
alter that particular manifestation of your past experiences
to fit the life you deserve. Don't do it out of your intellect
. . . that 12% area . . . do it out of your total being, the
subconcious vault of your experiences. Get in there and
recognize the "bad," dump it and focus on the magnificence of your being . . . your goodness . . . the area of life
in which you can truly play, fully.

Chapter 9

The Game of Life

As in any game, the game of life must be played. By "play," I mean the word in its truest sense. Webster defines play as, "to amuse oneself as by taking part in a game or sport," and that's how we must approach this game of life . . . by amusing ourselves, by having fun!

Unfortunately our puritan work ethic has allowed us to inherit an improper connotation of the word "play." It is instilled within us to "win" when we play—playing in itself is not enough. The work ethic tells us: WE MUST WORK TO BE PAID, AND WE MUST PAY TO PLAY! Hanging on to this rule has had tragic consequences in the entertainment industry. A famous actor, singer, entertainer or comic stands before an audience or a camera, doing exactly what he enjoys doing, and he is paid handsomely. How can this be? He's playing to his fullest extent, but whom does *he* pay to play? *He* is being paid to play, and his work ethic cannot handle it. The entertainment field is fraught with emotional breakdowns, divorce, heart attacks and suicides, not because the individual is more "talented" and thus more emotional, but because that person's entire background tells him he has to pay for his financial success. He evolves his own method of suffering in order to compensate for his success . . . for his guilt.

The mechanics of conditioned reality teach us that with every win there must be a loss, so we set ourselves up for life with this win/lose pattern. Believe me, you have to forget that! Life must be set up for each of us on a win/win basis. When I win, you win . . . when you win, so do I. There is no such thing as scarcity, there is only abundance and prosperity. Your joys I celebrate as my own. I don't have to rob you in order for me to have something . . . I don't have to make you lose so I can win. This means I don't have to compete with you. I can create my own and enjoy you creating your own. (Our next chapter will deal fully with the win/win.)

One young lady in my seminar challenged me on this win/win idea, in that she was deeply involved with a man, but unfortunately he was also involved with another young lady. He was dating both, but they were dating only him. To her, she was indeed competing with the other woman in an attempt to land Mr. Wonderful, and she couldn't understand, in this situation, how it could be anything but a win/lose outcome. The way she had it wired, if she won, the other woman would lose, and vice-versa. What made it doubly frustrating, she had decided this was the man she really needed in her life. Well, after we tossed out the word "needed" (not without a chuckle from her), she came to realize that even if the other woman "won" the man, she too was a winner because she could quit wasting her life chasing after someone who didn't want her. She also won by now knowing the kind of man she desired.

People waste so much time and energy thinking about their "problems" instead of dealing with their situations.

Life is not for thinking ... life is for living. If you are willing to play the game of life fully ... not working at it, not efforting ... then you will reap fantastic rewards.

Getting where you are today hasn't been easy. Our culture, our heritage, our social pressures are all potential debilitators. Life starts with the birth trauma and because we never learn to handle that, it serves as the first stone in a wall of barriers we erect during our life ... barriers which shut in our human potential and shut out the abundance of life within our reach.

Let's examine the trauma of birth. Here you are very comfortably ensconced in your own little apartment for nine months, curled up in a warm and liquid environment with all your needs attended to. You're aware of it re-member, since your subconscious has been operating for the past six months. All of a sudden you're evicted! No notice, no, "sorry, but we have to make some changes in your residence here," no nothing! Not only are you evicted, you are forcibly ejected, squeezed through a doorway that's too small and pulled by the head and shoulders. In an instant your dark and secure world is changed to one of blinding light ... to a world that is 26 degrees colder, full of loud voices and tension. While you're struggling to make sense of all this, you are lifted by the heels, your coiled muscles snapped straight and you are struck on the back. In some instances that umbilical lifeline is severed before you develop your own support system, before your lungs begin pumping air. In that moment of panic what must your mind be telling you? "To hell with all this!"

It is mind-boggling to ponder how mankind could go for centuries assuming this was the correct way to intro-duce another human being into the world. Why did it take so long for someone like Dr. Frederick Leboyer to come out strongly and shout to the world, "Hey, wait a minute ... there is a better way!" To me, the man is a saint!

In contrast to the old birthing method we have just covered, imagine a dark and quiet room, the mother and father both fully prepared for this magic moment, the child allowed to enter the outer world quietly and comfortably. The room is warm, soft music is playing in the background, the atmosphere filled with love for this new life beginning. The infant is gently placed on the mother's warm flesh, cradled, allowed to flex those cramped muscles on its own. Breathing starts normally, the umbilical cord is attended to, and the infant is gently lowered into a liquid environment the same temperature as his old address.

Buy a copy of Dr. Leboyer's "Birth Without Violence" and compare some of the photos. Examine closely the newborn being held proudly aloft by his heels, his face contorted in pain and fear. Then examine the picture of the infant, just minutes old, his face beaming in a beatific smile. Amazing!

I mention this new birthing approach to prove to you that all it takes for any improvement in the human condition is awareness, and putting that awareness to use. All Dr. Leboyer did was make us aware that every newborn infant is another human being, with all the rights and privileges we expect for ourselves. Let us now assume the entire world will get the message and stop all that inhumane treatment of another person, just because they're being born.

You can see by the birth experience that even as tiny little people we begin to make some incredible decisions about the life we are beginning. We have already been introduced to pain, fear and tension so we can relate to those emotions. In short order we encounter hunger, neglect, loud noises, confusion, dependency, you name it. Our mind is deluged with everything imaginable. As we grow, we are fed fact and fancy with no clear division between the two. On Halloween we learn extortion, on Christmas we learn the fantasy of "goodness," on the Fourth of July we learn to happily celebrate killing each other. If you want to get technical about humanity, you can even consider some aspects of Thanksgiving puzzling in that we pay tribute to the pilgrims who stole land from the Indians. Is it any wonder our inner being is so in conflict with the lives we are taught to lead?

When we are small we confront a world that is largely mysterious and we are not encouraged to investigate the mysteries around us. Instead, we are led to depend upon others to explain them to us. As an infant we crawl across the floor to investigate a spider busy spinning a web. Mother catches us as we sit there watching, screams bloody murder, snatches us away and crushes the spider with a newspaper. The spider had not harmed us and chances are never will, but the impact of mother's scream and panic, plus the picture of the spider, forever after makes spiders "bad." We are thus conditioned, and the child will always cringe and scream at spiders as though his mother had just shouted a warning. We now have a built-in fear of spiders.

Not being encouraged to investigate our world, we have to rely upon what others tell us, letting them train us. We are expected to take on their point of view as to the world around us. Initiative is frowned upon, yet children have a fantastically keen curiosity with an unlimited number of things they can look at, touch, taste, smell and so forth. Their urge to investigate is very strong, and they continue their desire to do so, despite discouragement from their elders.

Parents operate out of their own experience . . . they do the best they can. They teach us to stay away from lighted firecrackers so we won't have to experience the loss of a finger, but when the parents' own past traumas are passed on to the child in every facet of everyday living, something very stifling happens. The child encounters a dichotomy where the urge to explore is offset by the fear of doing so. Out of this dilemma comes the notion, "I can't win!" The child develops a "damned if I do and damned if I don't" attitude.

Very early in life the issue of "winning" is resolved. It's no longer about winning or losing, since it's already established that you can't win. What life then becomes is playing the game of life without losing too much. That's where the work ethic comes from, and why I stress time and again that the greatest single barrier to being fully alive is the work ethic.

Imagine this game of life as a huge wheel, and each spoke supports the rim from a central hub. To destroy the wheel, you can either dismantle each spoke, one by one, or simply punch out the hub. The work ethic has become the hub, where all the support originates.

Again, our attitude toward the game of life is no longer all about winning, but how can we lose the least . . . how can we keep from losing our shirt . . . the emphasis shifting from playing and living, to preventing a great loss. One of the things people keep criticizing me for is the use of the word "play," and I use it continually. I insist on playing at life and urge others to join me. Their criticism originates in the work ethic, in that "play" has come to mean useless activity and frivolity. We are supposed to pay to play, to give up a great deal to be able to play. What happens? We all get inured with this work ethic idea (it's almost genetic with us) that life's not about playing and having fun, experiencing pleasure and love, not even about succeeding, oddly enough. Even success is attacked, and I'll explain that more fully later. Life becomes all about self-sacrifice and work and efforting, "be serious, cut the frivolity," etc. It is the starting point for many of our trips into trauma.

It has come so far that entire industries are based on this philosophy. Look at the pharmaceutical field. There is no way you can talk about the human body and human emotions without talking about both. They're the same thing. How you feel literally translates into "what have you chemically done to your body?" Every time you experience an emotion, you must go into your body. You cannot experience an emotion only mentally . . . it has to be physical as well. Pharmaceutics is based upon what we do chemically to our body . . . the state in which we hold our physical being.

Look at the industry devoted to therapy. Since World War II it has become gigantic, based upon this, "I can't win so I'll just try not to lose my shirt" attitude. It is a tremendous producer of mental and physical ills.

I have very strong feelings about our own human potential and many accepted practices of therapy. I have actually been kicked out of group sessions because I was "uncooperative and destructive." The reason was simple, I just wouldn't take it seriously! One man had obviously settled on obesity, smoking, fear and nervousness as his own method of dealing with his "stuff," and was crying over unresolved hatred toward his dead mother. He was being given every agreement in the world . . . everyone was "helping" him unscramble his dilemma by reinforcing his "stuff." What I had to offer was, "Who gives a ____? What difference does it make? What are you going to do, dig your mother up and stomp on her bones? Stay fat and killing your lungs with smoke and crying because she didn't love you?" So, I was kicked out! I just wouldn't take the man seriously. I wasn't following the rules. I wasn't "handling" the man, patting him on the forehead, "dealing" with his "stuff."

Look, I know that within our minds are all our solutions, running along like buses on a boulevard. If you don't catch the bus it couldn't care less, it just keeps on going. You missed it!

Most people just don't know *how* to play. Every morning I go out running. Two friends join me and we all run at our own pace and believe me, we don't take it seriously. We are not "jogging" along prescribed lines, stopwatch in hand, we just run for the sheer joy of running. We decided one morning that we would transform the running course, which meanders around a San Fernando Valley golf course for some three miles. Popular with "joggers," the course is well peopled in the early morning hours. What we agreed to do was simply say "Good Morning!" to every person we passed. Not just "good morning," but a big, hearty, smiling "GOOD MORNING!" The reaction was tremendous. Here were people approaching "jogging" with the same scowling seriousness with which they approached any "chore." They were efforting, running to lose weight, to develop lung capacity, to tone muscles, whatever. They were all seriously intent on their "job" of running. So here come these three "nuts," obviously having the time of their lives, playing outrageously, waving and shouting a smiling, joyous, "Good Morning!" It was fascinating to watch. People would turn, stumble, lose their pace, stop and turn around, scratching their head. It was something beyond their comprehension. They were working, efforting, sacrificing and we were simply playing at it. We were all running, but *we* weren't doing it "right!" They really couldn't handle it. Our threesome also discovered that the lighter we took it, the farther we could go!

The way you handle the game of life is dependent upon whether you plug into the work ethic, which was invented by a "mind" to keep everyone uniform, i.e. "deprived," or whether you have the character of a bird. The only reason a bird flies is that he takes himself so lightly! If you take yourself lightly, you'll "fly!" Unfortunately, taking yourself lightly ... playing ... is not a part of the work ethic. By the time a child is six years old he is captured, bound and tied to the work ethic, with no agreement for investigation, curiosity, lightness ... for just natural, simple ebullience. You have to make life hard! You have to eat your spinach before you get the custard! All the lessons about making life "hard" come crashing down upon the youngster's investigative, adventuresome and playful tendencies, and all those tendencies are pure and natural. So who wants to play under these conditions? You end up not wanting to play! All you want to do is not lose too much.

Okay, how do you keep from losing if this is your background? There are a number of ploys our "I can't win" heritage provides us to keep from losing. Six of these cop-outs are classic, and were quite accurately labeled in the book, "Actualizations, You Don't Have to Rehearse to Be Yourself," by Stewart Emery (published by Doubleday

& Co.). Let's examine these six specific headings and expand upon them a bit.

Number one: *Don't Play!* If I quit, walk out, if I don't play, nobody can accuse me of losing. If I don't participate how will they know I couldn't win? The ultimate step in this direction is of course, suicide. That is the final "quit," in the game of life. Falling asleep is another way not to play . . . one popular in the classroom. If you fall asleep in a lecture, nobody will blame you because you were obviously tired. Not showing up is a way of not playing. You may be accused of being inconsiderate, of being selfish, but they can't accuse you of losing—you didn't play!

Take a look at your life and see how much of it has to do with not playing. How often do you just sit there, holding back, not expressing yourself? Of course your mind will justify it with good excuses like, "Well, I don't want to ask questions because I don't want to sound stupid!" Your mind is convincing you that you are stupid, and if you open your mouth you'll put your foot in it and thus you'll "lose." Rather than risk losing, you don't play.

We have a tendency to buy into some of the agreements our culture accepts in this area without even questioning them. Even some of our clichés are accepted at face value. A classic example is Abraham Lincoln's famous: "It's better to remain silent and be thought a fool than to open one's mouth and remove all doubt." Let's face it, what old Honest Abe was really saying was, "don't play!"

Number two: *Don't Complete Anything!* Now you may be called many things, but never a loser if you don't complete something. As long as you don't finish it, how can they say you couldn't do it? "They may say I'm inefficient, but at least they won't call me a loser. After all, if I had finished it, it would have been pretty good, but see, I never completed it so they'll never really know!" How many amateur writers end up with half-finished manuscripts and mere outlines simply because they refused to expose themselves to rejection—to failure?

Number Three: *Keep Others From Winning!* Here is where the human animal shines brilliantly.

If you would only take one-tenth of the creative energy you squander on keeping other people from winning and apply that to your own prosperity and abundance, you would be wealthy and supported and loved beyond your wildest dreams. Somehow we have it wired up that the way to keep from losing is to keep other people from winning . . . that somehow their winning or "making it" show us up as being a loser. Think of the times you have made others wrong. You were stuck in a win/lose, unfamiliar with win/win. Remember, the double-win doesn't exist in our culture. There's competition, there's jealousy, duplicity, all this other stuff we use to keep someone else from winning, but no win/win. No plus/plus. This is especially true of relationships in that if someone makes it with *us,* we assume a responsibility for that person and responsibility is ingrained into us as a burden. (Besides, who are you going to blame for all your mistakes if *you* are responsible for your relationships?)

There are people who actually create pain and call it love, stuck in the idea that loving someone makes them vulnerable and they will naturally be hurt. In our chapter, "The Rules of the Mind," we talked about Sally and her puppy-love experiences which led to the love/loss, love/hurt cycle. What makes you vulnerable is fear! Love makes you powerful and warm. Loving is like being the sun . . . it just keeps on shining. It doesn't *need* to shine, it just does and it will shine whether this earth of ours continues to exist or disappears. If mankind in all his craziness finally blows up this tiny dot in space, the sun will keep right on shining, in all directions.

Make every situation and every relationship a win/win. Fill your universe with warmth and aliveness so that people feel better for just being in your presence. Support their winning, don't keep them from it.

Number Four: *Destroy the Game!* When grandpa has us trapped in the corner of the checker-board with no place to move, we either tip over the board, or sure as hell think about it! Here is another cop-out move. If you destroy the game who can tell whether you lost or not? There are neither winners nor losers, so you can avoid a loss.

In the Alpha Workshop seminars we have a process which fully tests the individual's awareness. It's one which forces people to really examine where they've been coming from all these years, and one that drives the mind right up the wall. One man refused to return for the following day's session, simply because his mind realized there was a danger of not being able to run him anymore. That's the kind of fear we're talking about . . . the fear of facing your own reality. It enabled him to destroy the game, in this case by not playing, by not finishing, by making the workshop "wrong." How could he lose if he destroyed the game in his own reality?

Number Five: *Play the Nice Guy!* This is one we have already covered in our discussion of passivity. It is one which is rampant in our society, fully condoned. If you're nice enough, they won't have the heart to tell you you're losing and they'll let you play anyway. How often have you heard, "Oh, my God, how can I tell her . . . she's so nice. I just can't hurt her feelings."

Every morning Ethel comes over from next door for the ritual coffee break. So what if you have work to do, thoughts to think or places to go. Ethel is so damned nice, you just can't tell her to stay home once in awhile. So what you get to do is have coffee and danish and fury for breakfast. You swallow it all, refusing to deal with the hidden tyranny of that kind of niceness. But please recognize that while you choke on your fury, Ethel gets to avoid losing.

Something about games you must understand. All we do is play games and the more we play them, the more powerful they become. You can play being the nice guy in your effort to avoid a loss when you're in your twenties, but I will guarantee you, when you're fifty years old it will dominate your life. You will have surrounded yourself with people who dare not confront you simply because you're so damned nice. The monster you have created also means you get to baby-sit the grandchildren, even if you have other things to do. You get to work for this charity, for that church and you can't tell them to stick it in their ear because you have become your "act." You have become the personality you have constructed and the one they expect when they deal with you. "She'll do anything for you ... she's just so nice!" Great! Now you get to be oppressed because to set the record straight, you lose!

Number Six: *Become a Problem!* This one is really popular. You're doing poorly in school, not applying yourself to the studies and pretty sure you're headed for failure. Be a problem, get kicked out, and you avoid losing. Boy, did you show them!

A lot of husbands and wives stay together because one mate becomes ill. "You can't divorce me, I'm sick ...

I've got a heart condition!''

Becoming a problem is one of the favorite cop-outs used by alcoholics. How can they be accused of not playing life's game if they're an alcoholic? They can't help themselves, right? If their mood is not fitting into the party, they can just down a few more drinks and knock over the furniture. "Poor Charlie, he's an alcoholic, you know." Stop the game, I want to get off!

These are six ways in which you avoid having to deal with YOU. It's how you can get out of playing this game of life: Don't play; don't complete anything; keep others from winning; destroy the game; play the nice guy or become a problem.

Take a moment and see how this applies to your own situation and how you play the game of life. Have you been playing win/win or win/lose?

Like so many areas we have discussed, your attitude toward winning or losing is just that . . . an attitude. It's how you hold it. It's only data your mind has received, attached with an attitude and served back up to you.

Suppose I call you and we mutually decide to have dinner together, only you don't show up. I can come up with any attitude I wish. I can be hurt, I can be angry, I can wonder if there's something wrong with me, that you don't like me . . . I can bring up all my past rejections and go home with heartburn and dejection. I can also shrug my shoulders and sit back, enjoying my own meal and solitude. I can even "win" by realizing, since we hadn't discussed who was picking up the check, I may have saved myself ten bucks! It's how I hold it.

Say you go to a pastry shop to get a German chocolate cake. The one in the window is exactly what you want, only it's already sold . . . come back tomorrow and they'll have one. Okay, you win because you now know you want a German chocolate cake and you now know you can get it tomorrow! It's how you hold it.

If I fall madly in love with a woman who has all the traits I admire, and she chooses to marry someone else, I win! I win because I now know the kind of woman I'm looking for and she's out there somewhere. If I created one, I can certainly create another, and I'll find her. It's how I hold it.

To be able to play the game of life fully, you have to do away with the agreement that "play" means frivolity, irresponsibility, being non-productive and so forth. You must examine the world around you and realize every creature on earth plays. Playing is light, free, rapid motion ... it is pure enjoyment ... it is natural. It's also free because it doesn't cost anything ... there's no penalty phase. You don't even need anyone to play *with*, you can play by yourself.

Let's look at a so-called tragedy. A person is enjoying a bright future, a brilliant career, climbing a particular success ladder rapidly and he is involved in an accident which leaves him paralyzed. Now, this highly active person is confined for the rest of his life to a wheelchair. Somehow he makes the best of it, perhaps by becoming a top telephone salesman, or he develops such a keen awareness of individual potential he becomes a personnel manager. He again establishes himself as an active and participating member of the community. The secret lies in that the man still played the game of life, only aware now the rules had been changed for him. He understood the new rules and was not hating the fact the rules had been changed. Like the squirrel who lost his home and food supply, he set about doing what was required to get back into the game of life . . . doing his job.

When people encounter "adversity"—when the rules change—they're inclined to throw in the towel. It's so much easier to sit back and bring up all the self-pity, anger, resentment, wallowing in what isn't rather than developing what is. You see this in people faced with mandatory retirement.

I know a gentleman who was forced to retire at age sixty-five from a top executive position with a major oil company. They changed the rules as to how he could play the game. He didn't sit back and vegetate, stuck in rejection and moaning about his fate. He said, "Okay, I'll make up my own rules!" And he did. He took the money he had saved and purchased a funeral home! From an oil company executive to a funeral director. People thought he was crazy! They couldn't see why he didn't just take his pension and sit around waiting to die. What he did was reject the agreement we inherit about retirement. He operated the funeral home for twenty years, finally selling out when he was eighty-five. When I last saw him I knew better than to ask about his "retirement" so I only asked, "What are you going to do now?" Do you know what he said? He said, "Well Jim, I'm going to start a convalescent home for the elderly. I'm going to show some of these old people what it really means to be alive!" Beautiful! As he goes through life, he just keeps making his own new rules to fit his new circumstances, and he keeps on playing the game of life fully. He creates his own game!

Where does this agreement come from—this idea that retiring from a job is retiring from life? Let's go back to our analogy of the young child who had his own investigative, curious nature subjugated and was led to expect others to decide for him—others who "know better."

What does that child do at age sixty-five? He accepts his retirement from life because his natural curiosity has always been stifled. Since he has depended upon others for these decisions, he accepts the "agreement" about pensions, social security and retirement. Believe me, there is a direct relationship between not being allowed to investigate your own curiosities when you are eighteen months old, and succumbing to retirement—to giving up life.

The word "adventure" comes from playing in an area outside of your experience. Adventure does not come from knowledge, but from newness, and what makes life an adventure is your willingness to do something totally different, perhaps something you don't even do well. The old cop-out of, "Well, Fred retired and his job was all he knew how to do, so I guess his death wasn't unexpected," is pure insanity! Fred had a chance with his retirement income to support him, to attempt something entirely new. If he was a draftsman, maybe he could have opened a macrame shop or a book store or expanded one of his hobbies into a full-time occupation. You don't have to buy into the agreement that retiring means ceasing to function. You can still explore, investigate and find pleasure in *anything* if you wish to do it.

In the process of growing up we are taught we have to fasten onto something, make it our life's work, stick with it and then quit, sit back and wait to die.

When someone tells me their sixteen year old son doesn't know what he wants to do in life, I say, "Great!" What are those teen years for? For investigating, exploring, testing, experimenting, to find out what you really want to be. Give him until he's thirty! Society is going to stick him into a mold soon enough anyway. We have to get him into college, into a career, into the accepted pattern, get him into harness like everybody else, otherwise he's "sick" and not "normal." Conformity is the hallmark of being well in our conditioning. I'm sure at least one of your friends is looked upon as a non-conformist, and we pin a negative connotation to that because nobody is supposed to be that different ... that far outside the accepted social structure.

If children are allowed to explore they will become many facetted personalities with more interests than they have time to pursue fully. These are the people who will make their own new rules for their own new game of life when it becomes necessary to do so. These are the people who build convalescent homes when they're eighty-eight!

The norms however, are the social robots. They go to their job, they come home, they have their children, two cars, their meals, their television and two-week vacations and that's about the total scope of their lives. They conform to what everybody else is doing because that must be what's "right." Unfortunately, they in turn snuff out the spontaneity of their children, setting them up as conformists in a society that demands conformity.

Kids aren't supposed to get dirty, so mom goes around changing their clothes six times a day. They're not supposed to crawl around in dusty, dirty corners and cram the dirt into their mouth. So the child grows up resenting the restrictions and becomes a dirty housekeeper out of sheer rebellion. Look, kids are not stupid. Let 'em eat dirt a couple of times. Dirt is pretty low on the scale of tasty things to eat, and they'll soon get that. They're not dumb.

Earlier I mentioned that even success is going to be attacked, so let's look at that now. *The mind is trained to attack any demonstration of love, pleasure, fun and prosperity.*

Take a man who refuses to quit playing at life . . . who does not fit that definition of an adult: a child who forgot how to play. He is successful, can manage his affairs in three hours a day, takes back-to-back vacations, has a beautiful home and drives two expensive cars. Does he meet with approval for his successes, for his ability to earn his living while devoting so much time to playing? No, he meets with envy, criticism and harshness for not maintaining the established work ethic. His income of $60,000 a year doesn't excuse the fact that he's out there playing tennis, sailing, golfing, or lying on the beach in Hawaii. "It's just not right and there's something fishy about Edward, especially since his wife is so beautiful. He either inherited wealth and kept it secret or got involved in some nefarious business scheme he never talks about." Reactions are snide rather than supportive.

Playing at making a living and doing it in a way that gives you free time to enjoy life fully just doesn't fit the work ethic agreement.

Getting at these flawed agreements we inherit and making up our own rules is what increased awareness is all about. It's what alpha training is all about. Recognizing that, as children, we are instructed to be successful and make our parents proud of us, yet being attacked on every rung of the ladder gives us the opportunity to deal with that. Recognizing the agreements put upon us by our parents, by society, by our heritage, even our gender, enables us to transform the flawed ones and construct new ones to fit our desire to really play at this game of life. Believe me, the frustrations of attempting to fulfill a role society has programmed for you are completely debilitating. It is inherent in our nature to exercise our own initiative . . . to create.

If you and your spouse want to join hands, skip down the street and come back giggling and licking at ice cream cones, do it. Let the neighbors peek through their curtains with their sad head shakes and tsk, tsks. It has nothing to do with YOU.

Life is about living, not surviving. When you talk about the game of life, you're not addressing the agreements we buy into which destroy the game of life. When we adhere to the agreements we're brought up with, we change the game of life to the game of survival, only it's not a game anymore. You then live your life as though you were a permanent member of a party aboard the Titanic. The sea is too cold to jump into to escape so you're married to the fate of disaster. All you can "hope" to do is keep the ship afloat as long as possible . . . forestall the inevitable.

I define "evil" as simply trading in the game of life for the game of survival . . . surrendering your aliveness to take on the load of "agreement."

Playing the game of life fully is not without risk, but risk is just another word for adventure . . . again, it's how you hold it. We profit by our goof-ups . . . we learn. We undertake something entirely new, maybe sewing, and the bandage on our finger doesn't mean we failed. It means we were willing to do something out of our past experience to see how it would turn out.

If it's time for you to "retire," look upon it as releasing you from one game of life, and set about organizing the next game. We live, remember, in a world of abundance and your share of that abundance is exactly what you reach out and gather in for yourself.

Chapter 10

Plus/plus Equals Freedom

Having told you the game of life must be played on a win/win basis, let us now examine some basic rules and how the game of life applies to the mind, the body, the emotions and the inner being.

The game of life is played from one of four positions and I will show you how these positions always produce specific results when applied to such areas as relationships, responsibility, love, male/female role playing, addiction and guilt.

The only position which fully works is the win/win or plus/plus. In transactional analysis this is termed the "I'm okay, you're okay" position. Whatever position a person operates from, it is self-chosen, or in the negative sense, self-inflicted. We are thus talking about an attitude or how we hold the events which take place in our lives. Let's say you and I have a relationship. Regardless of what you do, *I hold* it as a win/win. It thus *becomes* a win/win. It is the context or the way you hold the game of life . . . a way to resolve whatever arises in the course of day to day living.

It's the way you resolve everything to enable you to get on with this game of life.

The result of position #1, the plus/plus (+ +) is your ability to "get on with it," so let's call this result "getting on with it." When you smash your car, it becomes something to be dealt with, so you can move on.

The + + position, when incorporated as a context for everyday living, transforms the experience of life from one of drudgery, burden and monotony, into one of adventure and spontaneity. When you deal with an event spontaneously you are dealing only with the event itself. The way you handle it is determined only by the facts which are pertinent to the matter at hand. This is not the way most people approach situations, however. The norm is to dredge up all the past garbage of our life, and our decision making power is guided then by past data, not current events. Your neighbor backs into your car and dents the fender. If he happens to be of a particular ethnic group, you trigger past negative experiences with others of that race or religion ... you berate yourself for again parking in the street and not your driveway ... you curse the fates and angrily whip your car in the garage, smashing the lawnmower enroute. You lose.

Using the same analogy, you can assume your neighbor has insurance so you'll be out no money ... the car still runs and will get you to work and the repair shop where you'll pick up a loan car or rent one (he's paying for it) ... the inconvenience is not a "problem," only a situation which you must deal with so you can get on with the game of life. You also win because you now know *always* to park in the driveway, not the street. It's how you hold it.

The + + position is not a position held by two people

... it is a single position, an individual attitude of one person toward the people and events in his life. Unfortunately this first position, this $+ +$ is held by far too few people in the world, especially in our own country. Ours is a culture founded on scarcity. It is a culture that centers on being afraid ... fear appearing everywhere around us. How well you function depends upon your level of fear. In our culture we are taught to be alienated from each other, founded upon competition, which comes out of scarcity. As a child begins to buy into this cultural agreement, to become affected by this attitude, he begins to create a minus $(-)$ in his life. From this he develops the number two position, which is a plus/minus $(+ -)$ ... in other words, "I win, you lose." In this second position, everything incorporates a loss, i.e., someplace, somewhere, sometime, there must be a compensation for winning, regardless where it comes from. This is the paranoid position of "I'm okay, but there is something wrong with you." A person in position #2 operates out of fear since everything he does means someone may rob him of something. Minuses cancel out pluses. The way a #2 position person resolves a situation is to "get rid of something."

Our notions of "good" and "bad" are so intricately tied-in to everything we do that in order for us to release something from our lives, we must make it "bad." We must somehow convert it into a minus to justify getting rid of it. It becomes impossible for two people simply to say, "Look, we have reached a level in our relationship where we can no longer serve each other, so I think we should give each other a final service. You go your way and I'll go mine and, out of love, I totally support you in going your way." That is a plus/plus way of dealing with the situation ... the okay/okay solution. Most people must make the other person "wrong" in order to end a relationship. They must create all sorts of heavy, bad feelings . . . go through a tremendous emotional trip . . . in order to get on with their own game of life.

The only person a position #2 can deal with is someone in the number three position, a minus/plus (− +). In order for these two people to play, they must play from opposite poles.

While the result or product of position #2 people (+ −) is "getting rid of," the position #3 people (− +) are busy "getting away from." It is the way they resolve things.

We were all born + +. We came into the world that way, and despite our birth trauma we were still basically all right with ourselves and everybody else, but as we developed the notion that others around us were separate from us and a threat to us, we began to realize that to accommodate everyone we had to play something other than + +. This is the basic game of "take away." I will take away what's bothering you and you will take away what's bothering me, and we'll play it two-handed. This is what so much of our society is based upon. But after playing take-away over a long period of time, we begin to create the number four position, the final position in the game of life, which is minus/minus (− −). When I lose, you lose. I'll blow your brains out and then I'll kill me. Remember the final scene in the movie, "Sayonara?" Red Buttons kills his mistress and then takes his own life. This was a minus/minus resolution, which is called "getting nowhere." These are not just intellectual ideas to play with, these are the four basic positions from which you choose to play the game of life. Which position you choose at any given moment determines the outcome. The outcome is built into the position.

Let me define position relative to the point we're making. Right now, I am facing you and cannot see directly behind me. My position only accommodates what is directly in front of me. To see what lies behind me I must alter my position ... I must turn around. Nothing has changed. I have only altered my position in order to examine fully all that surrounds me.

These four positions we are examining are the key to the game of life. Everything you engage in depends upon your position, or how you hold it. Whenever you act upon or discuss anything dealing with any aspect of living, be it money, sex, relationships, responsibility, whatever ... you have to make it very clear to yourself and others the position you're coming from. I must stress that these positions are absolute, they are not up for negotiation. You do not decide what your life will be, you can only assume your position and let life affect you as a product of the stance you have taken. Each position fosters a specific set of results, each result decided for you as a part of your chosen destiny. When you choose a position, your course is set.

Before we examine how these four positions affect specific areas of our life, let's diagram what we have established and what we will work from:

Position	Result	Relationships	Responsibility	Love
#1 + + =	Getting on with it	Freedom	Joy	Love
#2 + − =	Getting rid of	Alone	Duty	Sacrifice
#3 − + =	Getting away from	Troubled	Burden	Need
#4 − − =	Getting nowhere	Pain	Pain	Apathy

When you create the + +, the double win, you create freedom. This means freedom in the absolute sense of the word. There is no possessiveness, no hanging on, none of the manipulation which goes on in what we call love. There is complete openness and an allowance for others to be exactly as they are.

Anything, and please underline that word, *anything*, can be made a win/win situation. Regardless of past experiences you dredge up, there is a way for you to hold anything in order to make it a + + situation. The more you create the + + position, the more you create an expanding sense of freedom, a freedom which nurtures you. Most people connote freedom as cutting loose, spinning off at a whim without facing responsibilities. That is not freedom. That is a + − position, an "I'm okay, you're not, so to hell with you," attitude. When you create this second position, this + −, when you create other people losing so you can make it, the destiny you inherit is to be alone. Not with a meaning of solace where you finally get a respite, but alone as defined by alienation, as by occupying a mountain pinnacle by yourself, beyond the reach of others. When you assume the + − position there is no person in whom you trust. Everyone else is a minus, and you are the only plus. You become isolated and alone.

The destiny inherent in the − + position #3 is to be "troubled." It is only logical that in order for someone to fix you, you must have something wrong with you. As soon as one facet of your act is repaired, to maintain the − + position, something else must fall apart. It is the − + people who are continually shouting "help me." The minus/plus people are wandering around searching for the + − people, who are in turn keeping their eyes open for the minus/plus people. The majority of people you meet will fall into the #3 category. The next largest number are found in position #2. Roughly speaking there are three 3's for every two 2's. This is what keeps the crusaders, the evangelists going, all the − + people and their changing "needs" for help.

Now, the final position, the − − or minus/minus #4 position also has its product, and that is "pain."

Please get this: the way you conduct your life absolutely depends upon which position you select. For example, you will never find a plus/plus individual addicted to anything. Addiction does not occur in position #1. Addiction means to surrender your power to an impersonal force, whatever it may be. One of the fallacies that keeps appearing in many notions of psychology is that people are powerless. This is absolutely untrue. I have never met a person who was powerless. To the contrary, it takes tremendous power to keep screwing up your life. It takes enormous energy to continually create problems for others to solve for you ... to isolate yourself to the extent that nobody can get through to you. The difference is the use of power. In the + + position that power is utilized to support and nurture. In the other three positions the power is used to subvert and manipulate. This establishes positions #2, #3 and #4 as *control positions*. From these stances you attempt to control others.

Let's examine responsibility (see chart). Responsibility has four distinct points of view. The way people are responsible depends upon whether they create a world wherein they are joyful, motivated by duty, burdened or in pain.

The position you operate from has nothing to do with the reality of what goes on around you, it has only to do with how you hold what occurs in your life.

The sole purpose of my life is to create the space for people to arrive at the #1, + + position again. Once they get to + + they don't need to be taught anything else, for everything will fall into line as a product of their position. A + + person must give up all the minuses ... stop creating the minuses. You must stop creating scarcity, loss, bad, wrong, and simply *live*.

When I tell you your mind can drive you crazy, I'm talking about the mind's potential. If you are not truly aware, the mind will throw you a few zingers and knock you out of position #1. The mind keeps a continual propaganda barrage going to the effect that it is everything ... that the way you see with your mind is all that exists. That's a lie. What you see ... what you perceive ... is just a *part* of everything. What others see is also only a part of the whole. When you get all those parts together, only then do you perceive everything. The flaw here, however, is simply that the chances of getting all the parts together at one time are absolutely zero! Again, sitting here facing you, I cannot see behind me. If I turn to the rear, I no longer see you. That's what the game of life is all about. The game of life is continually expanding *toward* what is everything and the only position from which you can do this is the + +.

The moment you create a minus, you automatically move to position two or three.

Unfortunately, staying in the first position requires an almost Herculean devotion to purpose. Given the way people are trained, the chances are slim you will be allowed to remain in the + + stance. We are trained not to look, not to listen, touch, feel, and then not to be. By the time we get to "be," we're down in position #4, the − −.

One safeguard in the dangers of the #4 position: to

get there, one must spend considerable time bouncing between #2 and #3. It is in the second and third positions we get to exercise our awarenesses and correct ourselves, get rid of the minuses in our life and rule out the danger of becoming a − −.

When Charlie decides his life is fully working, that he is indeed in the + + position, he is continually tested. He comes home from work with his tastebuds tuned to a rib roast, only to find Helen still on the phone with the PTA members. Tonight, it's Kraft dinner and weiners. Somewhere, somebody is enjoying a rib roast and he's stuck with hot dogs and macaroni. He has a beautiful opportunity to get so hung up on what isn't instead of what is, he can drop out of the win/win position and become a minus/plus. He can also stay + + by knowing he has an opportunity to enjoy macaroni and cheese and weiners, and rest comfortably with the knowledge that tomorrow night he'll enjoy the roast. It's his attitude, the way in which he holds the events in his game of life.

As mentioned earlier, getting to #4 is achieved only after exhaustive bouncing back and forth between #2 and #3. #4 is a position of exhaustion, of tossing in the towel. All your addicts are found in the − − position. By addiction in this sense I mean when you are totally controlled by something impersonal, like alcohol. All you need to do to get an alcoholic functioning is raise him up the scale to the #3 or #2 positions. You don't have to take away his booze, just get him out of the − − where liquor is running his life. He'll stop being an alcoholic.

Read the autobiography of B.J. Thomas. It is an excellent book and a perfect example of someone in the − − position raising himself to a + +. The man went through a total transformation. Addicted to drugs, he needed the chemical intake to put him to sleep, to wake him up, to get him to eat, to stop eating, to handle his "stuff" and he was suicidal. All suicidal people are coming out of the #4 position. Whenever you become locked in a position of continual pain, you are in minus/minus.

As far as "curing" is concerned, this is a ticklish area. I don't talk about curing people, only getting them to raise themselves up a position on the scale . . . change the way they hold their life. The context of their being then becomes totally different.

Now at this point in the lecture someone always asks, "How can I get someone raised up to the + + position?" The answer is simple; *you* can't. If you are a + + and attempt to raise a #2, #3 or #4, you become a + −, the "I'm okay, you're not" position. The clue here is you don't "attempt" to raise someone up the ladder. Just go about your life being a + + and you become an example. Certainly you'll be asked, "Hey, what's happened to you, you seem so full of life and joyful all the time?" and then you get to serve that person by telling him/her where you're coming from. Not with an "I'm better than you" attitude, but with an open, smiling confidence that is natural when you're coming out of being. If that person gets it, beautiful. If he or she doesn't, then that's where *they're* coming from.

Okay, how does all this apply to the alpha state? Check the diagram and put a mental red line under the + +, #1 position. Now that line denotes a tremendous transition. Above the line is getting on with it, freedom, joy and love. Below the line are all the acts and traumas and pain of life. This line is very real . . . not just my way of separating #1 from the others. In the alpha state, the + + position is a functioning reality. You cannot reach alpha from below the line.

Many people, when they go into alpha begin creating

the same complex garbage they create in the conscious or beta state, and they "wake up!" Positions #2, #3 and #4 are the beta states of life, and represent a barrier to #1.

In alpha, there is no time, space continuum ... no right nor wrong ... there is only what exists and everything exists only as you create it. Below the line, reality appears totally different because our yardstick is the beta mind, the analytical mind, the critical faculty which is always evaluating, judging, inventing and so forth to defend a position, and that position is below the line. Position #1 requires no defense because it deals solely with what *is* ... the true reality of life.

The transformation from below to above the line is so complete that the firmly entrenched + + people don't even talk about it! They're so busy playing the game of life with joy and love ... there is so much aliveness and nurturing going on within them they have no need to stop and evaluate it. It's just *there* and that's the way it always is.

In alpha, these + + players create a totally friendly and supportive universe, joining with every person and situation in a plus/plus, devoid of manipulation, alienation, fear and pain.

Now please remember there is nothing "mysterious" about alpha ... there is no need to stop and "go into alpha" to handle a given situation. The practiced alpha brain-wave user develops a keen sense of when he is using alpha and not necessarily through a learned "process" or technique. I have been using alpha for years and I know exactly when I am creating the state. I cannot tell you *how* I know, I can only tell you I know. In alpha, I know I am all right. It is beyond words ... it transcends affirmation ... it is just "there." It is an extremely powerful sense. The best description I can offer is that it is a very quiet sense of self. An awareness of my inner being, rather than a sense of my mind.

It is quite difficult to tell people about the Alpha Workshop. It is so far beyond mere *words*. It is a tremendous prevailing sense of "self" and "self" becomes perfect. It is pure win/win. Using alpha in your daily life enables you to come totally out of being. You establish contact with your being only in alpha, with your critical faculty pushed aside. Your "being" is free and all powerful. Getting fully in touch with it may take you four years, four months, or four weeks, and I can promise you if you practice using it, you will learn to "go into alpha" with your eyes open, jogging down the street or in the middle of a sentence. It depends upon your own willingness to create the + + position ... to come out of being. Others will notice it and support you. They may not have the words for it, but they will transform themselves in your relationship with them. In the + + position everyone and everything totally serves you.

Now, let me anticipate a question your conscious mind is possibly chewing over, by giving you a question posed by one of the Alpha Workshop students:

"Jim, when you have a run of negative things happening, even though they serve you, ideally wouldn't it be better to have a lot of positive things happen too? And, are you personally progressing in a way so that eventually only positive things will happen in your life, so you won't suffer the pitfalls of those negative events?"

My reply was this: Suffering is a self-chosen emotion and "good" or "bad" are only ways to hold something. Whatever comes your way, without being judged or evaluated, serves you. It takes your own mind to make it

good or bad. A toothache serves me in that it tells me
something is going on with me. I can make it "bad" by not
dealing with it, by not taking care of it, by not handling it.
Any event in your life becomes negative through the way
you hold it.

When something comes up, you take care of it, complete it, and it's done. If you don't take care of it, it will
pile up and produce a "negative" effect upon you. You
need not get rid of it, you simply handle it. If you go
through life "getting rid of" things and people, your
destiny is to be alone (see diagram). If you keep "getting
away from" you'll be running all your life and be troubled.
If you don't do anything you're "getting nowhere" and
your destiny is pain.

In the + + position, *what you like or don't like is
totally irrelevant.* It does not mean I like you and you like
me. It means that you're all right with me the way you are.
Let's say you're a Grade-A bastard. It's your perfectly
natural right to be a bastard, and I'll support your life style
any way you choose to have it. I will even leave you and
it's still a plus/plus. You go your way and I'll go my way.
It has nothing to do with "liking" or "wrong."

A very close friend of mine devoted twenty-three
years to dealing with relationships from a + − position.
His first marriage lasted seventeen years, the second relationship covering six years, the last two of which were
living as man and wife. Neither ended in what he would
call the best of circumstances without the accepted pattern
of hurt and recrimination. It was only after he came to
terms with his position that relationships began working.
His next marriage lasted eight years, and when it ended it
was only because his wife had, through continuing her
education, obtained her Master's Degree in business,

reaching a new plateau in her own development. She had never before stood alone with any degree of awareness and confidence, and it was now her desire to set out on her own, totally, to see what life had to offer her as an individual. Their parting was amicable and my friend was fully supportive of his wife's desire to seek her own way. His reaction was not one of morbid regret or resentment, since his love was abundant enough to support her in her own happiness as well as his.

When he told his friends of the parting, and that he loved his wife sufficiently to allow her to search for her own purpose, he was accused of playing the martyr role, of not truly expressing his pain and anger. Society dictated there must be resentment and a feeling of loss, even hatred.

His wife went on to play her own game of life fully and is now an executive in the banking field. My friend found a woman who came so closely from his own ground of being, the two of them now enjoy a life so full of love and mutual understanding they both look upon their present situation as the high point in their lives, with each day becoming a new high of love and support. They play the game of life fully and joyously, and it shows.

Our lives consist of an on-going series of separate events. They only become negative when we have adjudged them to be negative. We adjudge them to be negative only because we refuse to handle them.

I mentioned that positions #2, #3 and #4 are control positions, so let's enlarge upon that. The word ''control'' is very interesting, because the dynamics of control are fear. You never need control anything until you fear it. If I control my feelings, I'm afraid of my feelings. If I have to control you, I am then afraid of you. Now, a teacher who has control of her class is far different than a teacher who is in charge of her class. Where you have control you have fear. Where you have fear you have intimidation, and where you have intimidation you have manipulation. Manipulation fosters retaliation and retaliation promotes upset and pain. These are all minuses.

All these products of control positions require that you come out of fear. In the + + position you are devoid of fear. Even if you're dealing with king cobras, fear does not dominate the situation. You know cobras so you know enough to respect them not knowing how *you* operate. You don't needlessly do stupid things with poisonous snakes. Although they're very definitely a menace, the + + means the cobra lives and you live, since you know how to handle them. If you don't manage a cobra, it will get you, fill your body with venom and you'll stand a good chance of dying. You can't "control" it out of fear, only gain mastery out of knowledge, respect and care.

I said, you never totally perceive anything from any position. It is like driving down the road in that you are never exactly on course more than perhaps 1% of the time. 99% of the time you are continually correcting, almost always in constant error. As you correct, you stay awake. If you fall asleep, you run off the road or hit something, and there is your negative. That's how you go through life, in an on-going series of minor and major corrections of all you encounter. You don't look for things to correct, you just correct as things occur.

Most people go through life looking for answers, but this precludes finding them. How much better to be a person who finds answers than one who searches for them. The basic position is then completely different, for when you find an answer you have to stop searching. If you are a chronic "seeker" you can't find the answer without destroying your position! The position of a seeker is position #3, the − +, "looking" for something that will help . . . something *outside* yourself.

Okay, let's go back a moment to relationships, since the + + position is most often challenged here, in that society dictates one party must lose when relationships end.

As a + +, you actually create and maintain your *own* small universe, and you give all others the right to be exactly as *they* are. In a relationship which ends, it is not necessary to say, "I don't like you," since liking is not the issue, only one of the peripheral effects of the situation. You don't even have to say the relationship is not working, since it is indeed working . . . it is successfully showing you that you and the other person do not belong together and you both win by gaining that knowledge. You get to maintain your + + universe and support the other person in going his/her way, *sans* animosity, bad feelings, etc.

When you are the source of your own life, you know what it is you are creating. When someone does not support your purpose you are free to let them go and create space for someone else who will support you. The barrier to this attitude is buying into the scarcity agreement, i.e. I cannot let them go because then I'll have no one. The trauma which accompanies a parting of the ways stems from the fear there will be no replacement.

Many years ago in the Santa Monica courts, a judge stated firmly that most of the divorces he was encountering were far healthier than the marriages. This was simply observing that something wasn't working, so you end it and open the space for something that will work for you . . . support you.

In our culture we have all become experts on suffering. The reason is simple. We learn that expending energy takes efforting and, since efforting is tiresome we choose not to do that. Since we can create suffering and pain without effort (it is totally easy to suffer since all it takes is an attitude) we must also realize we can create joy and prosperity with equal ease. All it takes is an attitude . . . how you hold it. If you have been studying the diagram, believing it is extremely difficult to get above the line to the #1 position, then please get this: *All it takes is an attitude!*

Now I am going to present something for your critical mind to jump on, chew up and leave you with your head pressed against the wall. *There is no way to go about making a change in anything.* Your mind will now tell you, "Okay, that's it. You can't do anything about anything, so to hell with it," and you get the chance to exercise passivity—step one in the four steps to incapacitation, remember?

Every event and every person is simply something to be dealt with. If you're a + + it is a golden opportunity for you to do something which will enable you to get on with the game of life, or if you're below the line, you get to make it a pain in the ass.

Your mind is basing its "to hell with it then" reaction on the absurd notion . . . the lie . . . that you are powerless. This is the below-the-line reasoning that you are "less than". . . less capable, helpless, feeble, weak, etc. You are not. What you must do to become any or all of these negatives is abdicate your own position of power. You must, by agreement, give it to somebody else.

The below-the-line positions are totally artificial . . . they are man-made. They occur nowhere else among life forms because the world is designed to operate plus/plus.

If you need any examples of + + in the natural world, study zoology. Tigers still devour antelope. Coyotes still eat rabbits. These are pure plus/plus relationships and through survival of the fittest, both species are enabled to remain strong and continue their existence. When man tampers with this position the naturalness of life changes.

Today there is a tremendous ecological red-alert because man has taken it into his obsessive, compulsive mind that wolves are "bad." Wolf populations in the Canadian north have been decimated through poisoning and shotgun traps. Consequently there has been such a tremendous growth in herd size among Canadian deer, elk and moose that forests have been stripped of vegetation. Now the forests themselves have become endangered. The solution was to import wolves from Russia and other sections of the north in efforts to return the natural ecological balance. Man is the only animal capable of "reasoning" himself into such idiotic situations ... the only animal sophisticated enough to "think" himself out of the natural + + position!

When you accept the + + as the natural position of life, you cease creating positions below the line and the only way they can come into existence is through your own power of creation. They are artificial, not natural. They don't exist until you make them happen.

When you accept that you are *powerful* and acknowledge you can handle the events in your life, you are home free ... you are in the + + position. You are now in alignment with the universe since plus/plus is the natural universal position. You now no longer hold anyone else responsible for your own well being.

Remember it is not a part of the + + position to be a proselytizer. The temptation is there since you are so aware. To attempt raising someone else up to your position you become a + −. Such efforts are not only ill advised, they are unnecessary. The moment you drop a + + person into a nest of #2's, #3's or #4's, those below the line will either leave, or turn into a #1. You saw this happen in the film, "One Flew Over the Cuckoo's Nest." One "well" person was dropped in among the "sick" patients and they began getting well. Jack Nicholson faked his insanity to get in, and once there began effecting cures among the mentally disturbed. Ironically, society's answer was to give Nicholson a lobotomy to make him like all the others . . . to conform to the "norm." The paradox of the film was the fact that the people running the institution were the "sick" ones!

In London, during the blitz period of World War II, an emotionally disturbed children's center was heavily bombed. The youngsters remained safe in a bomb shelter, but the structure was destroyed. Since they had no other place to put the "sick" children, they were literally "farmed" out to families in the countryside. With no clinical treatment available, each child in his or her own foster home was allowed to just simply "be." They planted gardens or milked the cows and helped on the farm. But do you know what happened? The kids got well! With no one to reinforce their garbage, that 10% area of their total circle, all they had to deal with was the reality of life as it was. They played their young game of life to the hilt. They couldn't run their numbers on animals since the animals didn't give a damn. If Johnny had an identity problem, the cow still had to be milked. If he didn't milk her the way he was instructed, the cow kicked him in the ass! Black was black and red was red with no intellectual analyzing to keep the children stuck in their "stuff."

Being forced by circumstances into the natural + + position of the universe, they could no longer support their positions below the line. You might say they learned from the animals . . . from the true nature of things!

Now let's examine responsibility further in the context of the four positions. Being responsible is the willingness to be the source of everything in your life, but when fitted into one of the four positions of life, you get to see how being responsible effects specific results (see diagram).

For someone in the win/win, plus/plus position, responsibility becomes an absolute joy. It is a joy for you to source your own life, not in the ha-ha sense of the word, but as defined by expressiveness. Expressing is letting go of. In the verbal sense, express means to cast out words. Even when you cry, you are joyful since you are expressing your sense of sadness.

When you go below the line the situation changes completely. When you are a + −, when you're out to make others wrong, what you produce is a duty . . . a "have to." In far too many marriages the motivation does not come out of joy, but out of duty. Society's agreement is such that after you reach a certain age one is "supposed to" get married. So, you select your mate out of a sense of responsibility to the norm, not out of joy. Under these circumstances, you stand an excellent chance of marrying someone who is also below the line. When you're coming out of a sense of "duty" and not joy, the tendency is to "settle" for something. The settlement ends the duty, and who the hell wants a duty?

If you're in the − + position, responsibility becomes a burden. You take on extra weight. It is no longer a question of joy and sharing, of contributing to each other, serving each other. Getting married from this position represents not an expansion of your life, but a contraction. In this position the husband has to give up bowling, his golf, his friends. He is suspect if he is enjoying himself since he's supposed to be a − +, the person who is "troubled" by relationships.

If you're in the − − position #4, you don't accept responsibility for anything because you're in continual pain, the same pain you are experiencing in relationships (see diagram).

When you listen to intellectual conversations about responsibility, listen carefully to discern whether the people are sharing with you the joy of running their own lives ... the joy of being the source of everything in their lives ... or whether they're simply coming out of a sense of duty; social or familial dictates of "have-to's."

In a marriage where both parties are − +, that relationship will be cemented by the minuses, not by the pluses. Each partner is content with the knowledge that, "I'm not okay but my spouse is," and their love reverts to "need."

If two plus/minuses get married I can almost guarantee you a divorce. You see, she is marrying him to improve him, and he is marrying her for the very same reason. They're both saying, "I'm okay but there's something wrong with you," and if that isn't a source of conflict, I don't know what is! This is the tragedy of our ultimate relationships ... that marriage, something that is potentially the greatest space maker in life, is turned into a union based upon minuses ... the defects ... the negatives.

Getting back to relationships, if one partner in a marriage is a + +, chances are extremely strong the marriage will work. As a general rule, a + + individual is not concerned with remaking anyone, thus the space is opened for the partner to transform. Oddly enough, the minute you don't give a damn, you begin getting results! When a marriage partner no longer gets support for his or her negatives, the minuses, they recognize it isn't working for them. When something doesn't work for you, you automatically stop doing it. You don't need someone to tell you it doesn't work, nor do you require someone to tell you what to do instead. Even though you may be totally befogged and befuddled, you will still think of some alternative to what you're doing and before you know it, it will work!

At this point in my seminars it is interesting to observe heads shaking in wonderment, striving to digest all this plus/minus data, but it is a natural consequence of our mind's power. What I am telling you is so beautifully simple, your mind doesn't want the eloquence of the material to come through. Your mind is attempting to put all this into something it can get its teeth into. It wants to chew it up, spit it out, and get on with its job of running your ass off. Your mind just doesn't want to accept this, simple or not.

The mind will tell you there is no such thing as this simple approach to the game of life. It will call it pure Pollyanna and Julie Andrews and Dick Van Dyke and Walt Disney and Bambi, that it's unreal. But these four positions *are* real. The + + position is the way the physical universe operates, with or without your participation. It is the source of getting on with it, of freedom, of pure joy and love.

Plus/plus is the positionless position . . . the bus running down the boulevard . . . and if you want to stop it and get on for the free ride, great! If not, it just keeps on going and couldn't care less.

Okay, let's now measure "love" with our four-position yardstick. When someone says "I love you," what is the sub-title all about? You don't really know unless you can discern their position ... where they're coming from. If "I love you" means you are absolutely free ... that the person saying I love you will share you with the world, then you have a plus/plus relationship. If, in a relationship, you have total support to be anything you choose to be, without restriction, you have a plus/plus going. One of the most beautiful experiences in a + + relationship is the feeling of pride. Being proud of someone is exquisitely quiet, without the huzzahs or bragging or strutting. When you are proud of someone you delight in standing back quietly and allowing the whole world to share the object of your pride.

Most people cannot tolerate someone else winning and this allows them no space to experience pride in the accomplishments of others. Their instinct is to cut in, steal some of the limelight, compete, take-away and say, "Well, if it wasn't for me, she wouldn't have become so successful." It isn't enough to just bask in Willy's happy glow because he made a hole-in-one, you have to be a + – and let everyone know it was because he was using your golf clubs. This is the everyday syndrome of, "If you think *you* had fun in Paris, you should have been with *me!*" You must keep others from winning!

When you let pride remain a + + in your life it becomes a fantastically beautiful quality. It is an inner-glow kind of elation ... a sharing of your abundance of love with someone else. You experience the thrill of someone *else* winning.

Usurping another's win position is often subtle enough to be commended. You see this on the Little League baseball or soccer field. "That's *my* boy!" The crowd's attention now turns to the father and his beaming pride, the son forgotten. The boy didn't make the goal or hit the home-run for his father, he did it for himself! When father swells with his inflated "pride" his son walks home in father's shadow, not in the brilliance of his own achievement.

When you move love down to the #2 position, it becomes sacrifice. Here is where we find the father who sacrificed his youth to support his parents, sending his own son out on the soccer field, and his son had better damn well make up for the old man's sacrifices! This is where you struggle to make up for some real or imagined loss by forcing someone else to succeed, and you call it love.

The last thing self-sacrificing people deserve is sympathy. They are manipulators of the first order. Sacrificing means you keep books, developing a highly refined accounting system whereby you make minute and accurate notes on every act of kindness you put out. By God, somebody owes you something! The destiny of a + − person remember, is to be alone.

When you sacrifice, you mortgage someone else to your own debt. You make someone else pay for your "stuff," or you at least attempt to. A self-sacrificing mother in a poverty situation, finding herself down to her last three potatoes to feed herself and her two children, will give all three to the offspring. She may become weak and ill, but by God someday she'll let them know how much she sacrificed! This is the "After all I did for you" syndrome. Listen to an argument between parents and children and see how much old sacrifice stuff comes up. Believe me, when your mind keeps using red ink in your ledger book, you will end up burdened by duty and alone (see diagram).

When we drop down to the #3, − + position we get the opposite of love . . . "need." In relationships this becomes deadly. Needs are interesting. First of all, any need you have will run you. When you enter into a needful relationship you must totally surrender all your power. The person you "need" will run you. When you make somebody else responsible for what you "need," you *transfer* your own power.

The only person who can satisfy your "needs" is you! When you give someone else a job that only you can do, you have a built in failure. Your need remains unfulfilled and you also now get to create hate or dissatisfaction against the person who failed you. It becomes an absolute no-win situation.

When you need someone for your own well being, the way that person thinks, feels and behaves determines how you think, feel and behave. The other person must do a certain thing to make you happy ... whatever *they* do determines how *you* feel ... so your needs cannot possibly be satisfied! Not by someone else! You are the only person who can satisfy you, but you transfer the job to someone else, making them responsible for you! Do you see the ridiculousness of this position?

Let me bottom-line this third position with a pure truth: You either *need* or *feed* a relationship. You can never do both. You either take from it or give to it. Unfortunately, regardless of the exchange of words, most people want you for themselves, not for you. They do not care how *you* feel ... they care how *they* feel about how you feel. They do not care about what you want, they care about what *they* want in regard to what you want. This is not "bad," it is just the way things are.

Now then, position #4, the − −, getting nowhere, "I'm not okay and neither are you," position.

Love in a − − relationship results in apathy. The very

best you will ever get is jealousy, the − − person bouncing back and forth between apathy and jealousy. This is a completely lose/lose position wherein you toss in the towel, pack it up. Your out is in a bottle of seconal or the top of a ten story building. Short of suicide, something strongly traumatic has to happen before a − − person is jostled out of his apathy. He just doesn't care anymore. It can be done, however.

As I mentioned earlier, addiction is a product of the − − position, but addiction is created because of its results. The alcoholic is attempting to gain the attention he "needs" to fulfill something he lacks. Isolate an alcoholic and he'll quit being an alcoholic.

There was a case in the 1940's where an Australian trading boat skipper, a chronic alcoholic, was isolated on a remote island to provide radio reports on Japanese ship movement. They didn't care if he was an alcoholic as long as he reported in, so they left him a huge supply of booze. When they finally came to take him off the island, they found him sober as a judge, ninety-percent of the booze left unopened! He had no one to run his act on, dump his drunken stuff on. All he had was hangovers, throwing up and nausea. Nobody cared. He couldn't affect anyone with his alcoholic stupor. It didn't work anymore, so he found something else: sobriety! The tag to this story is interesting also. When he returned to civilization he again became an alcoholic. He had his "audience" back!

Okay, we have established that relationships which work are found in the + + position. It requires two whole people to work. Below the line, when you have two halves coming together they do not make a whole, they simply remain two halves which stay together. They form a symbiotic relationship, each stuck in minuses and feeding off the other. Symbiosis comes from the Greek word for parasite. When you join two parasites their lives are spent attempting to consume each other.

If the way you are depends upon what someone else does, says or thinks, you are in a symbiotic relationship. If, however, you can be exactly who you are and are given the space to be whatever else you can be, and if the person who shares your life insists you be all that you can be, reach your full potential, then you have a love relationship. It may not take the form that Hallmark has made popular, or even that religion has made popular, but it will, however, endure and grow.

Now please do not be boggled with an assumption that this high pinnacle of the #1 position is so damned difficult to reach. All it takes is the recognition of the position you now hold and the creation of a new attitude. Again, it is how you hold it. It is simply gaining a new awareness and putting that awareness to work for you.

Become a plus/plus, get on with your game of life, and reap the benefits of freedom, joy and love.

Chapter 11

Myths of the Male Image

The material which makes up this chapter is a rather small part of the overall male image myth we examine in seminar form. The actual seminar covers two full days, with specific processes to accompany the lectures. It is an important area for investigation since it dictates the approach we take to the game of life, and our life encounters are direct functions of our sex roles. I'm not saying that's the way it should be, only the way it is in our culture.

This gigantic game of life we play is broken down into many sub-games. There's the inner game called marriage, the game of college, the game of high school, with sub-games called homework, football, etc. There's the game of parenting, fatherhood, motherhood, good-little-girl, bad-little-boy, thug, poor-thing and on down the line to encompass everything we do. They're all "games" we play within the master game of life.

All these games and games-within-games are divided into two *opposing* sets of rules. The first set is reserved for females, the second for males, and it's all one ridiculous, gigantic act.

Most of the males in the world function solely by the rules of the male game, and they are accepted and supported by our culture. There are a few females who operate from the male role posture, but they are scorned by both sexes. Nearly all females in the world play the game called "female."

What this acceptance of roles produces is alienation between human beings, simply because of a difference in plumbing. Those with outdoor plumbing have a certain set of rules, and those with indoor plumbing have a different set altogether. Our culture says the male is the favored one, and this is the primary myth. We are brought up to believe the male is the stronger, the more dominant, the supreme figure of the two sexes, and society supports this belief and perpetuates it. The female is accepted as the weaker figure, dependent upon the male for support, leadership and protection.

The man willing to play the male game will get an abundance of male agreement. If you're a woman, you will get practically none. The woman on the other hand, willing to play the female role . . . agreeing to be weak and helpless, sweet and gentle . . . gets full agreement from almost everyone.

The notion that men suppress women is patently absurd. The absurdity is based on the truth that all men are female oriented. With the exception of a select few, all males are run by women. They are woefully and hopelessly dependent upon women, which makes the female preeminent. Men present themselves as terribly romantic, pretending to be powerful. Women, in contrast, are frightfully powerful, pretending to be romantic. This posturing by the two sexes gets to be a bit silly.

To me, the tack the women's liberation movement has chosen is hilarious. I love it! I really think it's great . . . and it's crazy. The ladies are already dominant, already on top, yet demanding they get their full share. They already have it. All they need do is make themselves aware of it and acknowledge it.

Let's examine some actuarial statistics: In 1920 there was roughly an eight months' difference in the life expectancy between males and females . . . just about even. In 1977 it had reached the point where approximately 57 percent of our population was female—43 percent, male. If the progression continues, by the turn of the century the ratio will stand at about 70 percent female and 30 percent male. Since men expire sooner and the women inherit, where does this leave the power and wealth in the year 2000?

Why do men die sooner? Because males in our culture are programmed to self-destruct! All you need do is give a man something insanely dangerous, make it romantic, and he'll do it gladly! I'm not only addressing physical acts such as mountain climbing, wars and hang-glidering . . . I'm also talking about the insanely dangerous battles men engage in economically and politically. Men are perfectly willing to bust their ass, even kill themselves to show women (and other men) how powerful they are. So, Frank takes off in his rickety, home-made aircraft with everyone cheering, kills himself, his wife gets the insurance money, goes on a cruise, meets and marries another self-destruct male who is heavy into building a business or parachuting. Women are oriented toward self-preservation . . . too intelligent to expose themselves to ridiculous and unnecessary dangers, especially when they have no idiotic macho image to protect or enhance!

I am going to show you how this all works, and I

openly invite anyone to prove me in error. If you can really show me where I'm screwed up, I'll get off of it . . . I'll cancel the "Myths of the Male Image" seminar and never give it again. Okay? Then here we go:

Every single person has a powerful female imprint. Why? Because every human being is born a woman. This is something you cannot refute. We are all born from, and as a part of a female. The maleness or femaleness is determined by the genitalia *after* we are born and by subsequent input from our environment.

The medical community, finally, after boggling for centuries over the human condition, is beginning to acknowledge that maybe, just maybe, there is some prenatal influence . . . that a tiny, unborn child, living and growing inside the body of a woman, just might be influenced by that woman. There is so much evidence to substantiate that all babies are influenced by their mother prior to birth, how could it be any other way? The man has no direct influence over the unborn child. Indirectly, yes, but mother's attitude toward father is generated by mother, regardless what father does, and the baby shares that, right along with food, water and everything else.

This brings us to an unarguable fact: the male's first prolonged point of view is female. Males thus have a very powerful female imprint, and they get to share the point of view of females for roughly six months before they are born. Then, upon his birth, the male child is given to a female to be cared for and nurtured. Mother becomes the lifeline for both the male and female infant. The male infant is fed, clothed, cleaned, amused, played with and educated by mother. The female imprint is further strengthened since the point of view being generated by the growing male/female child is almost totally female. Father is relegated to the role of a funny smelling stranger who pops in at six o'clock in the evening, usually too tired or busy to do more than play with the infant briefly in a superficial way. Unfortunately, one of the strongest influences father has upon the child is to discipline as he fulfills his role in the, ''You just wait until your father gets home'' syndrome. Father thus becomes only a secondary influence on the male child ... mother predominates.

What happens next is almost as traumatic as the birth experience itself! Around the age of five or six, the male child is abruptly served notice he must cease and desist his relationship with females. What is the worst thing you can call a small boy? A mama's boy!

Here we have a male child who has had nothing but the female point of view all his life, including six months in the womb, suddenly told he must give it up! The female child is not expected to do that. To the contrary, the girls are encouraged to be like mommy ... to cook like mommy, smell like mommy, dress like mommy, etc. And little girls want to do this because, after all, this big lady is the model for daddy! Emulating mommy will teach girls how they can catch a guy like daddy themselves! Obviously he went for her, so the daughter decides to study mommy so she can be just like her. It's a terrific role model because society offers no resistance to such motivation. It's fully encouraged. The girl gets to continue being mommy's little girl and daddy's little girl. The boy however, must now be daddy's big *man,* although he has no training for this role within his female imprint. The male child now must copy this funny smelling, six o'clock stranger about whom he not only knows very little, but someone he has also come to fear! Somehow he must begin formulating his father's point of view, something completely out of context with his past experiences. What he learns rather quickly however, is that his father's point of view is actually formulated by *mother!*

What happens when daddy comes home and supper isn't cooked? Daddy doesn't eat! If mother doesn't iron daddy's shirts, he doesn't have a shirt to wear. The male child sees mother remaining the dominant role figure, only nobody admits it! It all appears rather puzzling to his young mind. All of a sudden dad insists he play with other little boys, but unfortunately these other small boys are going through the same confusion! He's stuck with it however, because "boys don't play with girls!"

For approximately the next ten years everybody agrees that the male must have only male friends. If he's caught playing skip-rope with girls, he's called a sissy. This is the foundation upon which is built the universal "fag button" nearly all males have. Boys are supposed to torment girls, tease them, pull their hair, toss mud on them and destroy their dolls and thereby become red-blooded males. The highest compliment the small boy can receive is, "He's a man's man!" It's okay to pull wings off a fly, smash a frog, slug a buddy, all the neat things boys are supposed to do . . . but deep inside of them they have this strong female imprint going which is in conflict with society's dictates. For ten years or so the female imprint is not only *not* being nurtured, it isn't even acknowledged.

When I think of young men stomping through their teens and twenties with this society-dictated macho stance, completely ignoring their strong female imprint, I recall a visit to Disneyland. Remember the jungle boat ride? Standing forward at the wheel, guiding the boat through narrow channels filled with menacing automated figures, a young man fires blank cartridges and spins the wheel to protect his passengers from ferocious lions, alligators and wild head-hunters. The ladies love it, giggling and screaming as he cleverly steers the boat to safety. Completely ignored by all is the fact that the boat is perfectly controlled by rails under the water. The skipper could sit and knit "blue booties" and the boat would run along safely by itself.

Just as the young boat skipper goes through his acts of heroism while the automatic control of the boat is ignored, the typical macho male performs his acts of maleness as demanded by society, and his powerful female imprint is equally ignored.

By fifteen or sixteen years of age, the male is a "man's man," chasing around with the guys, into motorcycles or cars or rugged athletics . . . all fully supported by our culture . . . and all of a sudden something else becomes the measure of his masculinity: Women! Those funny smelling strangers with long hair and flowery dresses who have been receiving all his taunts . . . the ones he's been taught to avoid for the past ten years! Now, he no longer gets agreement for hanging out with the guys. He can't walk hand-in-hand down the street with his buddy, he must do it with one of "them."

All these years, while junior has been going through this confusion, girls have not been uprooted once. They're still mamma's girl, still daddy's girl, still hanging out with their childhood friends, getting together, playing, laughing at how silly boys are, etc.

Suddenly the guys start hanging around girls like bulls in a cow pasture. All the past joking about the difference in plumbing now becomes a drive force among males and the ultimate goal turns to one of conquest. Boys aren't taught to talk to girls, really communicate with them, only to tease them, ridicule them, dominate them. Boys can "respect" them, but it doesn't rule out lying to them or manipulating them, since they're only girls. Since they're taught they are more dominant, bigger, stronger, better and far more important than females, young males do not offer themselves to young women as equals, they in effect inflict themselves upon them. After all, they're "supposed" to be the boss. So the way they take care of their natural and growing sex drive is through conquest. They have to "get a woman!" The insanity increases to the point where, if they can't get a woman, they must lie about it. "Hey, Eddie, did you get laid last night?" You can bet Eddie will say yes, even if they just had a coke after the show. That kind of conquest becomes a measure of his manhood. All his buddies know he's lying but it doesn't make any difference, the role is more important than reality. Besides, all the while Eddie's lying about it, his buddies are rehearsing their own tales of sexual prowess.

We now reach the point where a young man must be measured by his sexual domination of females, so he's out there maintaining the image as the whole world watches and supports his performance. He must be very virile, very athletic and keep up the ridiculous posturing. He must be "hard," not only in an erectile sense, but in his manner as well. (God help a man if he "can't get it up" anymore. It is such a strong fear that most often the fear itself is the sole cause of impotence.) So he flexes his latissimus dorsi, takes bigger steps, lowers his voice and eyelids, talks a lot of ladies into the sack and he's home free. He's accepted . . . he's playing his proper role. He lacks only one important ingredient in his make up: HE DOESN'T KNOW HOW TO RELATE TO WOMEN anymore. He can break walnuts in the crook of his arm to impress the gals, but he can't talk to them.

It gets crazy! If you're a football player, the entire stadium will rise and give you a standing ovation for finishing the last quarter with a broken collarbone. You'll do it for good old dad and the gal friend and all your buddies, disregarding the fact that you could puncture a lung and lose your life. That's what I mean by crazy. You get all sorts of agreement for this kind of behavior because you're maintaining the male image, even though deep inside there rests that dormant and powerful female imprint. It's there, even though it has never been acknowledged or nurtured.

Out of this grows the preposterous notion of the male "ego." *There is no such thing as the male "ego," there is only the refusal to acknowledge the female imprint.* No male can deny its existence. It is there and must be acknowledged and dealt with.

Taking Junior away from his mother's side and tossing him into the boxing ring or out on the football field without maintaining his contact with the female imprint is like taking a five year old German boy out of Berlin, raising and educating him in Japan for ten or twelve years, and then dropping him back into Germany and saying, "Okay, talk German!" But that's the way our society handles the male child.

A boy is not supposed to play with dolls. It's okay if you call it an "action figure" or a tin soldier, but don't ever call it a doll! Yet, a man is supposed to be a kind and loving father. How is he supposed to know how to hold a baby and "play house" when he gets married, when it's the last thing he's allowed to do as a kid? Women play house endlessly and their mother role is simply an extension of their life experience as females. Mothers bitch at their husbands for not pitching in and helping out, but they just don't know how! They're also too damned proud to admit it and afraid to ask, and can't verbalize their fears since men aren't supposed to be afraid! They can get drunk and angry, smash the car up because they're just big boys anyway, but they can't express their fears and inadequacy in the father role.

One of the crazy things our mind does is measure *everything*. (Even our greeting is a measurement, i.e., "How are you?") When it comes to sex, big is better, longer is better, deeper is better . . . the mind goes absolutely nuts! It is totally into how many numbers. So after a guy has tallied his required number of conquests, proving he's a real he-man by spending years going hump-hump in the dark . . . proving his sexuality by the number of notches in his belt . . . he sets out to find the "pure" one, some lady who isn't "damaged goods." He has to get married . . . not necessarily wants to, he *has* to . . . because you know what they say about guys who get up around thirty who aren't married. There's that old fag-button again.

What a man gets to do now is hustle out and prove he's a real man again by getting married. He's never been allowed to play house, never been allowed to play with girls . . . he can't talk to them. He knows he must dominate them, get them in the sack, and all women are supposed to do is feed you. That's it! In fact the feeding aspect of relationships is fascinating to examine. Look at the female notion of what men are, i.e., "The way to a man's heart is through his stomach!" Terrific. What that really says is, "Feed the idiot and he won't attack you," because that's all boys want to do anyway. Everybody knows if you feed a boa constrictor a pig it will lie quietly for a couple of weeks and won't eat anybody else. So feed your man and he won't "attack" you . . . but keep your eye on him anyway, just in case.

Look what happens to the newly married husband . . . he goes around patting his growing waistline saying, "Look, she loves me!" Ask a man how he likes married life and he'll pat his stomach, look down at it beaming and say, "Great!"

Just for fun, if you'd like to do an experiment, take the eating ritual out of your relationship and see what happens. You'll realize just how much our lives revolve around this eating mania. "Let's get together for lunch . . . come over for dinner some night." It's as if there were a little Jewish mother down inside us constructing our entire life around the ritual of food consumption.

What happens when a man asks a lady out for a movie and says he'll pick her up about eight o'clock? Eight o'clock! That's too late to eat! "I didn't say anything about dinner, I just asked you out to a movie!" Chances are the cheap-skate is going to be out of a date. It gets so that, if a couple doesn't have a plate of food in front of them, they don't know what to do with each other. "Let's get to know each other, come over to my place for dinner."

Most people are run by this eating ritual. There are some, truly life-centered people, who put their stomach into a different perspective. Some men stick an apple in their pocket and go out running, or eat out of a desire for nourishment rather than companionship. Women grab a quick salad and go play golf or bowl. But put women and men together and the first thing they do is *eat!*

Okay, back to our accepted male/female roles. Men are not supposed to have men friends . . . they're supposed to give them up when they get married. I have been best man at friends' weddings eleven times and I am no longer close friends with any of those eleven men. When a man marries, the wife will either insist or cleverly arrange it so that her husband's single men friends go out the window. "I do not want my husband chasing around with a single man, because you know what you guys will do when you're left alone . . . unfed."

Women are more fortunate. They have friends who date back to childhood. Their bridesmaid and school chums are still a part of their intimate circle. Not only are they allowed to have their friends, they're *supposed* to have them, because that's who they *talk* to. The husband doesn't want to listen to all that girlie stuff.

So women are supported in getting together and they get to share. Men don't know how to share, so they aren't allowed to have friends. If two males get close it pushes society's fag-button, and that's something no male in this society will risk . . . being called a fag or gay. To hell with actually *being* gay, just the mere suggestion that a man *could* be or *might* be is enough to make a man shake hands no longer than three seconds, talk in a louder voice and take up weight-lifting.

This isn't common in all cultures' but certainly in ours. In the South Pacific Islands it's a different story. In Tahiti, when a woman gives birth to a second son, it is common for her to strive again for a girl, but if the third child is also a son, quite often she will raise the boy *as* a girl. He will be dressed as a girl, groomed as a girl, and learn all the household tasks as if he were a daughter. The reason is simple. She needs somebody to help around the house, so her son becomes a "Mahu," a boy/girl, and it's not only okay, it's beautiful! There's no stigma attached, no fag button to be pushed . . . "Rauu wants to be a girl, so let him be a girl . . . I'm going fishin' on the reef." Nobody cares. In the Tongan Islands the same thing exists only the man/woman is called a Fafafini.

It is also quite common to see two men walking down the road holding hands. In Tonga the men are huge, majestic figures and American tourists are often seen snickering in the background at the sight of two burly men walking happily, hand in hand. Tongans couldn't care less. They might come to our country and witness two smiling men slugging each other on the shoulder and wonder why two men who appeared to be friends were beating each other!

If men have a fag button, the ladies are also triggerable because they have a fat button. You can question a woman's sexuality and she'll laugh in your face. She has nothing to prove, so to hell with it. But call her fat, and it's a whole different story. A woman will diet, jog, join a health club or go on a fast to avoid being called fat. A man will do *anything* to avoid being called a fag. These are the two buttons most people push, either directly or indirectly. Men lean on the women's fat button, which is about as close as they can get to challenging a woman's sexuality ... while women manipulate men via the macho image men establish for themselves. Challenge a man's masculinity and he'll come through with flying colors. "Sweetie, you couldn't possibly carry that big trunk down to the basement, could you?" Look out, here comes the hernia!

The sad part of all this sex-button pushing is the resultant alienation. The more we trigger each other, the more we grow apart. The more men maintain their male image and the women their female image, the more difficult the avenue of communication.

It is the man who suffers most from this alienation, since he not only loses contact with and closeness to women, but as a husband he also loses closeness with his male friends. Close male friends are just not condoned. He can have a golfing or bowling "buddy," usually someone approved by his wife because the friend is also married . . . but the friend cannot be single. He cannot be "trusted." The male is thus alienated and isolated from any close relationship, while the female retains hers.

When this happens, when the man loses his close friends, his wife usually assumes their place. When a man gets to the point where he tells his wife, "Honey, you're my best friend," that relationship is in dire straits, because he has shut off every avenue of nurturing except for that of his wife. Somehow, some way he'll extract his revenge for being forced into that admission, because what he's really saying is that his well being is now totally her responsibility.

In our culture it is the female who is responsible for maintaining the relationship, not the male. This not only places a very heavy burden on women, but they must mask and submerge their powerfulness. They must now play the great earth-mother role to this macho fool who has no friends. They must become totally responsible for what happens in the relationship. In such instances, the man becomes more "little-boy-like" as the years go on. This accounts for the strong matriarchal role of women in grandparental generations. Grandpa ends up toeing the line to grandma's running of their lives.

This is the lunacy which comes out of relationships where the two partners maintain the myths of their male and female images. The wife will ultimately rebel against being forced to become the power figure and her husband will finally rebel against her assumption of that position. The wife's rebellion usually takes the form of getting fat and complacent . . . the husband's way of getting back at her is by having extra-marital affairs. There are the "good times" of minor sharing and familial routine, but that role-product undercurrent eventually erodes away the basis upon which their marriage is founded.

A woman attending the "Myth of the Male Image" seminar once asked me what she could do to get her own husband to recognize his female imprint . . . make him aware of the fallout from his attempting to maintain the male image. My reply was simple; nothing.

An aware wife can display concern, she can communicate, but she can't change her husband by efforting to do so. When she takes responsibility for him "getting off of it," it doesn't work. Referring back to our win/win chapter, when she attempts to "make him better," she becomes a + −, and he will resent it.

Men go to therapists, not because they want to, or desire help, but most often because they're about to lose their woman. She has threatened to leave him if he doesn't go. He's still being run by her. Very few men take our seminars at the Centre because they're eager to learn; most are driven here by their wives or sweethearts. This is still the woman playing the mother role, and as long as she is willing to so perform, he'll continue to be the "little boy" who will manipulate her any way he can in order to hang onto her.

It doesn't have to be this way, however I caution women that if they have a relationship with a male and wish to let him free himself of all this maleness idiocy, they must be willing to lose him in the process. Most women are unwilling to do this.

You see, in order for you to cease being the simpering female role figure, you have to start being a whole person, and this just may trigger his female imprint and scare hell out of him. In this event he may fight back with, "You're

becoming dykey . . . I can't take these aggressive women
. . . you're much too powerful for me, etc.," and run off to
find somebody who'll take care of him.

I love women who are powerful. My reaction is,
"Great, let's play together! Let's create, let's have some
fun together!" I am too old to baby-sit! By far the majority
of women find this attitude reprehensible . . . all they wish
to do is take care of me . . . feed me, iron my clothes, clean
my house. If I tell them I don't want that, they tell me I'm
too old . . . too set in my ways. That's not the case! I just
want a real, live person I can play with . . . not another
mother. I don't require a female to tell me how to dress,
how to look, how to cook. I happen to be a marvelous
cook, and this offends women no end. They love to eat my
cooking, but they hate the fact I'm a good cook!

I've said you can be "concerned" for your husband,
but that does not include mothering. The concern which
comes out of true love is space-making . . . it gives the
other person freedom to be as they are. If I "love" you,
what I am really concerned about is your relationship with
you, more than with me. Until *you* know who you are, how
can *I* know who you are? I am willing to offend you, even
at the risk of losing you, if I can somehow create the
opportunity for *you* to deal with *you*.

One day a small boy came running up to me on the
street, nearly in tears, asking if I would please tie his shoe
so he wouldn't be late for school. I first asked him if he had
been instructed in how to tie his own shoe, and when he
replied that he had, I refused to tie his shoe. "But I'll be
late for school," he cried! "Great," I replied. "Then you
get to arrive at school with an untied shoe!"

How in the world is he ever going to learn to tie his
shoe if everybody does it for him? AND HE'S A LITTLE

KID! Believe me, there's no difference between that small boy and the thirty-five year old husband who is completely at a loss if his button isn't sewn on or his meal isn't prepared. Give him a recipe book and a skillet and say, "Here, go to it! Enjoy!" Women refuse to exercise this kind of independence because they're "supposed" to do it for them and besides, he might leave!

I have shown you that we already have a female dominated culture, and that the fact is denied by both sexes. The macho male posture certainly won't let men admit it and women won't jeopardize their image of the weak and helpless female by acknowledging their tremendous power.

Perhaps by the year 2000, the cold, hard statistics will prove the power position of women in our society. There is an excellent chance that the awareness will come too late, however, and instead of males and females meeting on a common ground, sharing on an equal footing, the result will be only a reversal of roles and the tragedy will continue.

Chapter 12

Guilt

In Chapter Two, "Our Human Emotions," I said we would examine "guilt" more closely. Guilt has popped up throughout this book since it is one of the most common emotions with which we tend to plague ourselves. Notice I said we plague *ourselves*. Guilt is never inflicted upon us, it is always a product of our own mind . . . again, the way we handle things.

Guilt is never an original emotion, it is always a function of two others. All three are tied together . . . never separated. Where you find the third, you will always find the other two . . . where you find the second, you will always find the first.

The first in this debilitating trilogy is fear. Fear is called the *flight emotion*—when we become frightened our desire is to run. Fear is the one emotion which dominates the lives of everyone in our society and what makes you different from others is simply what you fear and to what extent you fear it. The more fear you have, the more you are run by the world around you.

Our whole society is devoted to making us all afraid. If you don't believe that, examine television commercials for but one example. Commercials are fear oriented in that, if you don't buy those gooey blobs of Twinkle-Toes pastries for your kids, they won't love you! The implication is that feeding your kids 38% preservatives will somehow endear you to them. We fear for our acceptance by others when we're talked into breath mints, deodorants, beautifying cosmetics, false hair pieces, padded bras, etc.

When we encounter fear and don't resolve it . . . when we fail to handle it and get on with our game of life . . . fear becomes sort of recycled and appears next in the form of anger. Anger is what we call the *fight emotion,* for obvious reasons. I admit to having some psychologists argue this point with me, a few even becoming "angry," perhaps out of a "fear" of my being correct. The fact remains however, that we human beings cannot become angry unless we are frightened. Anger must be supported by some form of underlying fear.

In our culture, anger is something definitely frowned upon. We use every source at our command to make anger "wrong." Consequently we tend to get stuck in it . . . we can't release it, deal with it, lest we be condemned.

Referring to our last chapter briefly, there is one exception to this right-to-anger attitude of society: Men are allowed to be angry providing they make up for it later. Women, on the other hand, are never permitted anger. When they display anger they are called shrews, hostile, bitchy, etc. It goes totally against their assumed image of sugar and spice and everything nice. Accordingly, women go around a lot more pissed than men! Their anger is manifested in other forms of behavior, some of which can become deadly.

Since we are not allowed to manifest anger, we suppress it and it too recycles and reappears in the form of guilt. Take anyone who feels guilty, scratch below the surface and you will discover what they're pissed off about. If you dig below their anger you'll find what it is that frightens them. Guilt is a pure laminate emotion, always lying beneath the other two.

Guilt is termed the *freeze emotion*. It's the one which motivates us to do nothing . . . just lay back and let it brew . . . and it is truly deadly and debilitating. If you feel sufficiently guilty about something, the mind tells you it isn't necessary to do anything about cleaning up your mess. Guilt is an extremely powerful force and as I mentioned earlier, it isn't what someone else runs on you, it's what you create for yourself.

Surely you've had experiences where you were playing, coming out of joy, and said something that triggered somebody's button. Their reaction was one of resentment and since you obviously caused their ill mood, you triggered your own guilt. But what happened really? You meant no harm, you were being playful or joyful, and did not offer any action which was negative. Their *reaction,* which was a product of their own data bank, is what triggered their mood, not you.

When you create guilt, you make it all right for you *not* to do anything about the situation. This is not something we invented . . . it comes out of our collective training. It's the basis of our penal system in that, if you feel bad enough, long enough, you're considered rehabilitated. Using this analogy, we are all in jail. We make guilt our prison, with imaginary emotional bars to confine us, keep us locked in.

Guilt is the emotion we relate to the past and it

provides us with all the reasons why we "can't" do something. If you're stuck in guilt and wish to make sure you'll *never* get out of jail, you can project yourself forward and contaminate the future . . . and that's called *worry*. Your position looks like this:

$$\text{Guilt} \leftarrow \text{You} \rightarrow \text{Worry}$$
$$\text{(past)} \qquad\qquad \text{(future)}$$

Worry keeps you stuck in jail from now on, and guilt keeps you stuck because of what's in the past. Now, if you are exceptionally clever you will take "worry" and disguise it in such a way that everyone will applaud you . . . you will call it "hope." So if you now "hope" long enough you can stay stuck forever!

The way to get unstuck of course, is to take care of your guilt by digging down through the layers and taking care of what it is you fear. If you're guilty because your relationship with your mother is screwed up, then perhaps your anger is directed at her for closing off communication through the generation gap, and if that's the cause of your anger then, just maybe, your fear is simply that of not receiving her love. When you understand that she is coming out of where *she* is because that's *who* she is, you can then accept her and she will love you for it. You can quit attempting to squeeze her into a form that will fit who *you* are. Once you lose your fear, there's no cause for anger and no by-product of guilt.

Guilt is a weird form of comfort. Examine the quality of your own life. Most often, the moment you get uncomfortable your first inclination is to split . . . get away from it. The mind tells you not to face it, not to deal with it, just leave it. All this does however, is validate the prison you've put yourself into. Imagine being in prison and having the jail door left open. All you need do is walk out, only where you are is dark, comfortable, familiar, and if you walk out *there,* it's bright and unknown. When you put your ass on the line and decide to gamble on being uncomfortable, you walk out! Sure it's uncomfortable, but once your eyes become adjusted to the bright light you look around to find it's a whole new world out there! You have improved your position by a willingness to deal with discomfort.

Guilt is one of those uncomfortable ways of being comfortable about things. It is necessary to seek out discomfort, not as an enemy but as a companion. Through new experiences, adventuring into unknown areas, we grow.

Comfort is addictive, and like all forms of addiction we find ourselves being run by something completely impersonal. Our lives revolve around being comfortable, not only in the physical sense with water beds, plush davenports and overstuffed chairs . . . but in the emotional sense as well. We will not jeopardize our comfort by telling it like it is . . . by dealing with our emotions and ridding ourselves of situations which become "problems."

Let's examine relationships, relative to comfort. Every relationship starts off with good feelings and good intentions, but eventually some form of discomfort settles in for both partners. Unless you have two plus-plus people involved, the minute they begin feeling uncomfortable in the relationship, they begin to manipulate. Rather than face further discomfort by "bringing it up," they go into their individual acts . . . they pretend, they lay back in silence. Each partner recognizes this in the form of additional discomfort and the solution then is more acting, more covering, more pretending. Acts are polished into a fine art and yet both know it still isn't working. It is then they seek out the marriage counselor, but sadly, at least in my own experience, many marriage counselors only train people to manipulate each other better or differently.

There is a wide gap between communication and explanation. To communicate means to share each others' essence without forcing the other person into a defensive position . . . just putting it out there. People have communicating wired up as "output," but that's only half of it. In order to follow our universal law there must also be "input." People fail to really communicate because they don't *listen* to each other. Most of the time, when people are talking to you, you are busy formulating your reply . . . rehearsing your own material . . . or as is most often the case, dragging out your "ammunition." This is coming out of "explanation," not communication. It is now a desire to make oneself right. Communication is communication whereas explanation is a form of argument.

Communicating has more to do with understanding than with words. Most communication seminars concentrate on building vocabulary and expressing yourself but they don't teach you to communicate. You only become better equipped to manipulate others with better words.

Explanation is a function of resistance and a validation of the plus-minus position. If I am explaining to another plus-minus more powerful than I, it forces me into a minus-plus position, and I now must work even harder to explain myself since I have to come out "right." Out of this comes argument and we end up talking *at* each other. While I'm busy explaining me to you, your mind is busy rehearsing you. To communicate one must listen to what's going on with the other individual. One person puts out and the other takes in. When we begin to "explain" ourselves, we stop that natural in/out flow.

Getting back to our subject matter, guilt is all inflow and no outflow. It's the freeze emotion. You simply sit there and feel bad, assuming if you feel bad enough, long enough, you won't have to do anything about it.

It is common for an argument, disguised as a discussion, to end when one or both parties become "bored" with it. Boredom in this case is a result of never "getting it." It comes from resistance, not really listening and understanding. Boredom is an inefficient expression of anger in that you're actually pissed off . . . no longer listening . . . formulating what you wish to put out and not taking anything in. You're not communicating . . . you're so preoccupied with making your point of view known you don't listen to the other person. This is a true plus-minus position and it is a trap. Plus-minuses don't listen to minuses, they only listen to other pluses, only they don't know any!

When you go to a Swedish movie you're dependent upon the English sub-titles to understand what's going on. It's also essential to read sub-titles in communicating with others since the words we hear are only a small part of what a person is really feeling.

Let's imagine a small boy, report card in hand, rushing into the kitchen with a beaming smile and shouting, "Hey Mom, look! I got an 'A' on my report card!" His mother is not yet finished waxing the floor and her son tracks a half-dozen footprints in the wet surface. When she says, "Oh that's just *great,* Joey," it's with the same tone and inflection she would use if he had just spilled his soup on the carpet. The words she used were exactly appropriate, but her sub-title was totally different. Joey doesn't hear the words, he hears her mood and knows he's in the dog house. What she said was, "That's great, Joey," but what she communicated was, "Dammit, look what you did to my floor!"

If you're good at reading sub-titles, you can take the loveliest, flowery letter in the world, read between the lines and come up with a message entirely different from the one contained in the words.

One of the greatest experiences you can have is being with people, when what you say is where you're coming from. They may wonder at first what strange planet you came from, since they've never met anyone who spoke English with English sub-titles, but they won't have to wonder who you are because you are totally open. You are fully communicating . . . no longer presenting your act in place of truth.

Assuming this stance of openness . . . this plus-plus position . . . frees you of fear. When you are truly coming out of being . . . when you acknowledge that inner sense of being "all right" with yourself . . . you do not fear misunderstanding or vulnerability. Without fear you are not triggering that chain reaction into anger and winding up with guilt. Without guilt there is no freeze emotion, no stopping of progress and growth. You are free to adventure into new areas, test new ground, expose yourself to discomfort for the experience itself. It is how we grow and become complete human beings.

Out of the contentment which comes from being totally attuned to who we are, comes that tremendous feeling of self-love. Out of love-of-self comes our ability to share that love with others, and that opens the space for us to be loved and nurtured in return.

Remember, all it requires is an awareness and putting that awareness to use. It's that bus running down the boulevard on a regular schedule. You can stop it and get on for the ride, or watch it pass by. The bus (which is life itself) doesn't really give a damn which option you choose. Life just keeps on going, with or without you.

Chapter 13

The Five Deadly Sins

Common in our Christian-Judaic culture are the seven deadly sins: pride, covetousness, lust, anger, gluttony, envy and sloth. These "sins" are looked down upon as the source of all our evils. Actually, these seven sins are more traditional than powerful. They represent a sort of bogy-man or bugbear in our mind . . . an imaginary influence to keep us on the straight and narrow path. If we consider the exact definition of "deadly," these seven sins don't really qualify.

There are *five* sins however, which are indeed deadly. They claim lives minute by minute, especially in the United States. (Webster has a word for this ridiculous hectic pace our society sets for itself . . . one which drives people into ulcers, heart attacks and premature death. The word is Americanitis, defined as a condition of excessive nervous tension brought about by the fast pace of living indigenous to America.)

The five deadly sins are like tiny, electrical charges we fire in our brains . . . small, powerful attitude explo-

sions which literally kill people. The five always go together, inseparably joined like links in a chain and like
those multi-lens auto stoplights, they fire in chain
reaction—one triggers the next until number five fires and
it in turn activates number one again.

Anyone into the study of heart disease, though they
may use different terms, will basically support this prem-
ise. A number of cardiologists, aware that I teach this
reality, have sent patients to my self-hypnosis seminars to
get in touch with the way they conduct their lives.

This deadly fivesome lowers our level of consciousness and creates what we call tunnel-vision, which in turn
produces many of our stress-oriented ailments, thus lower-
ing the life expectancy.

The first deadly sin is called the "hurry-up." We're
all familiar with this one because all our lives we have been
told to "hurry-up." As children we are told to hurry up and
get up, hurry up and eat our breakfast, hurry up and do our
homework, etc. This tremendous mass of commands we
experience is filed in a specific part of our data bank, and
every time we get a hurry-up command, whether self-
imposed or sourced from outside influences, we tap into
this highly coercive force we have filed away. Because
coercion always produces resistance, we tighten up, clamp
down on ourselves in such moments and inflict fantastic
stress and strain upon our own mind and body. Our resistance comes out of an inherent awareness that the hurry-up
is not a natural part of our being.

All the ads and articles about the stresses of daily life
are garbage. It isn't what we encounter which inflicts the
stress, it's the way the mind deals with it. We do it to
ourselves . . . we stress ourselves with the hurry-up.

I compare the hurry-up with driving an ordinary

sedan down a freeway at its maximum speed of 125 miles per hour. Use your imagery to picture such a scene—an ordinary sedan on an ordinary freeway with ordinary traffic. Now, please describe what the driver of that speeding car is like. Simple. He is tense, he is perspiring, he has a knot in his stomach, his sphincters hanging on for dear life. He is totally dominated by the road ahead . . . not the road he is immediately traveling over, but the road ahead . . . out there. When you have your hurry-up plugged in you're pushing so far, so fast, you are oriented far ahead of your position. It completely takes you out of the "now." You know that traveling at such a tremendous rate of speed demands every ounce of your attention and ability and you are completely locked-in to what lies far down the road, hence the tunnel-vision. Your periphery becomes unimportant and goes unnoticed. You're screaming down the freeway at over twice the speed of everyone around you and your very life depends upon concentrating solely on what lies ahead. You can't enjoy the passing scene, you can't enjoy the ride, you can't hear the radio over the roar of the engine and you can only steal a quick glance at your instruments because of your dodging in and out of normal traffic.

Suddenly these "normal" folks, driving at 50 or 60 miles an hour become a threat to you. They're perfectly sane, enjoying life as they ride, and you're crazy as a loon traveling 125, only you have *them* wired up as being nuts. Can't they see you're in a hurry? Why don't the idiots move over! You lean on the horn, scream out the window and hurtle through space.

Some people call it impatience, but it's just another way of saying they're plugged into that hurry-up drive. All it is really is you exerting tremendous coercive pressure upon yourself, pushing yourself faster and faster as you speed through life. They also call it hypertension, but it's the hurry-up. Your mind is racing, your body is not keeping pace, so your blood pressure shoots up in its effort to produce enough push, enough force to support that coercion. If you suffer from hypertension, you're stuck in that first deadly sin, the hurry-up.

Interestingly, people who snail along through life, moving very slowly, taking their own sweet time with their assignments are also plugged into the hurry-up, only they are fighting against it, resisting it tooth and nail. They take the opposite path. When their mind shouts, "Hurry-up," their energies are concentrated on total resistance. Oddly enough, such people who are methodical, slow moving, unemotional are also subject to high blood pressure and that is the consequence of the built up stress from simply resisting so damned hard.

Please understand, the hurry-up is not just a thought . . . it is psycho-physiological. You're pumping adrenalin like crazy and that has specific physical results. Your body can never keep up with your mind and it is this adrenal efforting which cuts our lives short. (If the body could maintain the mind's speed we would all be comets!)

So that's the number one deadly sin, the hurry-up. You can spot it by the tapping foot, the itchy and jittery movements, the chewed fingernails and torn napkins. They're sitting still physically, but running wild internally. It's why cardiologists continually plead with their hypertension patients to SLOW DOWN! The heart is only muscle and can only handle so much stress, then it goes "snap!"

So ingrained is this hurry-up motivation, our minds will always attack graciousness, relaxation and ease as being some form of laziness, slothfulness. When someone declares, "I don't take vacations, I haven't the time for that sort of thing," they have their hurry-up plugged in.

Okay, with our hurry-up plugged in, running us crazy, we come to the number two sin: "be perfect."

When you're hurtling down the freeway at 125 miles per hour, what is your one concern? For God's sake, DON'T MAKE A MISTAKE! The reason is simple: a mistake is deadly! One split-second error on your part and you die! Everything around you becomes a mortal threat so your primary thought is not to make a mistake—be perfect!

Maintaining our analogy, you're already under fantastic stress because of the speed of travel, and now here comes added stress in your fear of making an error. Your goal of being perfect, of making not even one small error, borders on paranoia toward everyone around you. It's a simple fact of physics that the faster you do something, the greater the chance for error. As well as being stressed by your situation, you also stress yourself.

The mind always sees mistakes as "bad." They're a black mark against you . . . you'll fall from heaven . . . you have to hide it, alibi and remove the stigma of error, etc. A mistake in reality is only a part of our experience: "Hey, I goofed. I apologize and won't do it again." Period. That ends it and you get on with playing the game of life. People who have been triggered into the second sin of being perfect become super critical, not only of themselves but everyone else. They have no tolerance for error, whatever. These are the people who unconsciously grind their teeth while they sleep, and that comes from gritting them together all day long. Every error, every goof they encounter is a sub-trigger which attacks their be-perfect.

Now number three fires into action. The third sin is called the "please me." The "me" does not mean the person. "Me" is the demand of the mind of the person. The mind gives the command. Not only do you have to drive the car fast and not make the slightest mistake, you must do it exactly "as I showed you." It isn't you, telling you, it's the mind ... the recording ... the data bank telling you.

The hallmark of the please-me voice is, "What will other people think?" Now the danger, the fear, is not only that of doing something "wrong," it is also what people will think because you didn't do it "right." You're afraid you won't do it the way you were told to do it.

When you're plugged into your please-me, it isn't a fear your child won't take the garbage out ... it's the fear he won't do it the way you told him to. That his way works becomes unimportant. What is important is that he didn't do it the way you told him to do it. You see this clearly in mothers teaching their daughter to set a table or iron. "No, I told you to iron the collar first!"

I encountered an example of how we carry over some of these please-me traits from one generation to the other when one of my students puzzled why his newlywed wife always cut both ends off a ham before she baked it. She said she didn't really know, except her mother taught her that way. Her husband assumed it had something to do with releasing the juices, or allowing the fat to run out, so he asked his mother-in-law. Her reply was the same ... her mother also had instructed her to cut both ends off the ham before baking. Finally, he pinned down his grandmother-in-law and she said, "Oh that? Well, when I was raising my daughter, the only pan I had to roast a ham in was too small, so I always trimmed a bit off both ends so the ham would fit, that's all!'' Makes one wonder how important some of these please-me habits really are.

Am I doing it right? What will the neighbors think . . . what will the people in church think of me? Will I get the approval? That's what the please-me is all about. Again using our analogy, you're hurtling down the freeway, flat out, under tremendous stressful conditions, your tunnel-vision only allowing you to focus far ahead . . . panic-stricken that you might make an error . . . and to top it off, whatever move you make has to be done exactly right to get the approval of everyone. All those around you are a royal pain, they have become obstacles and God help you if *they* see you make a mistake!

Bang! In triggers deadly sin number four: "be strong.'' That translates to simply, "don't feel.'' Not only are you doing this insane thing, but you must act as though it does not even bother you. Men have an extremely strong propensity for this particular sin. Men are universally be-strong players and their number four trigger is almost continually activated. They have to pretend they don't feel it, it doesn't bother them, they don't care about it, all the macho garbage of their upbringing. Men are not cool, unemotional, fearless, pain-protected bundles of muscle and fortitude, they just think they have to act that way because they're supposed to. What's going on with our motorist, be he a male, is the true picture. He's sweating, tight as a drum, terrified with a knot in his stomach, just like any other human being under like stress conditions. He hides it because he has to "be strong.''

Men have maleness wired into hardness. They pride the hard muscles, the hard abdomen, the jutting jaw, Captain Courageous posture, but while they do this they also form a hard attitude. Their assumed role denies them the opportunity to let it all hang out . . . to cry . . . to be emotional . . . to feel . . . to really experience all the natural emotions.

Our motorist now has to take this huge ball of tension and swallow it, pretending it isn't there. Here is where deadly sin number five fires and it is called: "t-r-y harder."

"Try-harder" is the flip side of the hurry-up and all it does is trigger you right back to number one again. The harder you "try" the more you effort and the less you accomplish, so again it's hurry-up! It's not unlike nailing your shoes to the floor before a foot race. When you "try" harder you totally scuttle any chance of winning your objective.

If I have pictured these five deadly sins so that your mind lies defeated at the prospect of correcting such a hair-trigger chain of physical and emotional disaster, let me give you the highly complex solution. SLOW DOWN! Sounds complicated, doesn't it? In truth, you already have the solution at hand. You know that in order to be poor you must know all about being rich so you can avoid it, right? If you know about being perfect you must also know what it means to be ordinary. To know about speeding you must know what it is to go slowly. All you need do is move over to the other side of the spectrum . . . not completely to the opposite side where you become the laid-back, never-care, lethargic individual . . . but just over *toward* that side. Slow down!

Everyone has all of these five deadly sins to a greater or lesser degree, and becoming aware of it will enable you to tone it, tame it to provide you with a natural method of taking care of your everyday situations . . . one which will not land you in the hospital or a cemetery plot. Instead of being run by it and succumbing to such stress-related ailments as heart attack, hyper-tension, high blood pressure, ulcers, migraine, colitis, etc., what you can do is simply shift your position toward some semblance of normalcy . . . slow down. If you know what it's like to hurry up, then you know what it's like to take it easy, so just begin doing it. Instead of hurrying up, being perfect, pleasing your mind, being strong and "trying" harder, you can ease up, take the "wrong" out of error, please yourself, be soft as well as hard and quit efforting.

Examine your daily routine and see how tightly you have things scheduled together. Scheduling this tightness is how people keep their hurry-up plugged in. Plan your day not to fit your mind, but your own well being. You'll find some of the things you do can be put over to tomorrow or left in someone else's hands. If your immediate reply is that you have no one around you whom you trust, then take a look at the life you have created for yourself. When you tame your be-perfect and get out of that super-critical role, you learn to delegate authority to others, discovering you really don't have to do everything yourself.

Hurry-up people have a tendency to surround themselves with incompetent people to support their own self-destruct pattern. They can then refrain from delegating authority and have that delicious feeling of being imposed upon, triggering the hurry-up so they can be perfect and do it like they're supposed to and thus be strong so they can "try" harder. That is not how the game of life should be played.

If you reflect over the concepts presented in the other chapters you find that here again we are simply talking about an attitude. It all comes right back to how you hold things. And, again, the solution is gaining an increased awareness and then putting that awareness to work for you. All this hinges upon motivation and if you are motivated to improve your life, gain mastery over your own life, then just begin doing it.

Getting all those reins back into your own hands . . . ceasing all the manipulating and being manipulated by others and external events . . . knowing you indeed have an "act" and that it is perfectly all right as long as you know it *is* an act . . . getting rid of that tunnel-vision, hurry-up drive so you can fully enjoy the "now" . . . all this will enable you to play this game of life fully.

It is an exciting awareness to finally realize you never again need leave your life to chance.

Chapter 14

Hello Murray? It's Me!

By now you are well aware I use the word "play" continually. It is our approach to the game of life and the attitude which brings joy into all our encounters and relationships. Before we conclude with an explanation as to how you may reach the alpha state, I'd like you to play with me now in using your own imagery. Remember, your imagination is not only more powerful than knowledge or reason . . . it is also one heck of a lot of fun to play with.

For those of you old enough to recall the golden days of radio you must surely remember the great "Jack Benny Show." When Benny made his transition to television it took me some time to equate what the screen displayed with what was lodged in my imagination. For some reason, my mental picture of Jack Benny's "vault" and the plaintive "guard" who protected Jack's wealth, was nothing like the image I saw projected on my TV set. With only the radio voices and sounds to guide me, I had constructed my own scenery and visualization of characters and, to me, they were far more vivid than the TV "reality."

At any rate, this is the kind of imagination I want you to use now. First of all, think of your mind as a two-level office building. Upstairs, in much smaller quarters, is the conscious, 12% segment. This is the one you feed all your thoughts and perceptions into. Whatever it receives is automatically shunted downstairs to a rather large area . . . the subconscious, 88% "vault." This lower room is one huge data control center, complete with memory discs, reel-to-reel data recorders, switching panels, communication circuitry and any number of direct tie-lines to every part of your physical body. Here is where you have stored everything you have encountered since the age of 3 months (after conception). High on one wall is a huge video-read-out screen, sourced by everything you think and perceive.

Imagine now, seated before a complex looking control panel, just as Benny's guard sat outside the vault, a rather pleasant, calm figure whom we shall call "Murray." Murray is the guiding genius for all this data processing equipment. At his fingertips are all the controls necessary for activating whatever you flash on his screen in the form of directives. Murray cannot think or reason . . . he is simply your obedient servant who happily brings whatever you put on the screen into fruition.

Murray is pretty busy, resting only when you retire, go into alpha and give him the night off. During your waking hours he is continually in movement, but smilingly doing his job, speedily and efficiently.

Now then, let's say you're a man sitting home, relaxed, reading the paper. As you scan the baseball scores they are simultaneously passed down from the upstairs conscious level and flashed on Murray's screen. Obediently, he shunts them over to your data bank for statistics, just in case you want to remember them someday. All of a sudden, you sneeze! It could have been a bit of dust tickling your nose or just an involuntary twitch of a muscle, but nonetheless, you sneeze. You drop the paper quickly and exclaim, "Dammit, I've got a cold!"

Meanwhile, back in data control, Murray's screen flashes, "COLD!" If we could slow down Murray's reaction time (which is instantly) like an extremely slow instant re-play, what he does would look something like this:

Murray punches a direct line to the body chemistry. "Hello, Body? This is Murray. Listen, our guy's got a cold . . . just flashed on the screen. What's our white blood cell count right now?"

"Lemme check," says the body. "It's normal. No chance of infection right now."

"Forget that," says Murray, "he says he's got a cold, so you'd better knock off enough white cells so he can have it. Better tell the eyes to water a bit and get the nose to start running too. While you're at it, call the nasal passages and maybe they'd like to swell up a bit."

"Okay, got it," says the body! "Anything we can do to help!"

So as you sit there scanning the paper, your physical body begins to alter its chemistry and involuntary machinery. You grab for a Kleenex, wipe your eyes and nose and bemoan, "How in the hell did I catch a cold!"

Okay, let's see what Murray does with emotions. Suppose you're a wife who has been snitching a bit from the grocery allowance each week, putting it in a secret, seldom used sugar bowl. You don't really know why but it could have something to do with that fantastic new cookbook Helen told you about. In any event, hubby is nosing around one day looking for tea bags and discovers twelve dollars and sixty cents in the sugar bowl.

"What's this for?" he asks.

("Hello Murray? It's me. My husband just found my secret piggy-bank. What do I do?")

Murray's screen flashes and, again in extremely slow motion, we see him punch up "Guilt." Up on the screen flashes you, as a small girl, standing in the kitchen with jam all over your face, your hand in the jar and your mother grabbing you and paddling your rear end. Murray punches another button and the scene changes to you, on your honeymoon, standing hidden behind the bathroom door frantically attempting to hide that small blue box of tampons as you hear your bridegroom's footsteps approach.

Murray picks up the phone. "Hello, Betsy? This is Murray. Listen, all that kind of stuff is really private. The bastard had no right nosing around in your own domain. Chew him out good, it's none of his damned business!"

So you verbally lambaste the old man, yakking away, tears welling, stomach tense, and just for the hell of it you toss in, "Besides, I was going to buy you a present!"

Boy, did he get it! Now *he* gets to feel guilty! The poor guy backs off, pissed, but too guilty to display anger, and retreats to the garage workshop.

Meanwhile, Murray is rubbing his chin thoughtfully, mulling over that comment about your plan to buy hubby a present. "Where the hell did she get that from?" he puzzles. He switches up some old re-run reels, scans them closely, and finds no stored data dealing with a planned gift. All he sees is some flashes of a leather-bound cookbook!

"Hello, Betsy? This is Murray. Listen, I don't buy that thing about planning to get your old man a present. That's hogwash and you just said it because you were angry. Anyway, now you're gonna have to feel guilty 'cause you know that was really a cheap shot."

So, Murray's data flows back upstairs and into your mind as an attitude: guilt. Now you get to brood over the situation, sniffle away some tears, slam the silverware drawer, breaking the handle, and wishing to God you could muster up the courage to go out to the garage and tell hubby you're sorry. You remember the paddling mommy gave you so you exercise your passivity and do nothing. You just stand there at the sink, biting your nails.

Okay, thank you for the loan of your imagery. Do you see now the tremendous power of your own subconscious?

Whatever you hold to be true is binding upon you, and it is you who must do the holding.

Whatever agreement you make with how you think or how you feel, determines how you are.

"Hello Murray? It's me. Hey, how am I?"

Chapter 15

Reaching the Alpha State

In referring to the alpha state, the state of self-hypnosis, I have emphasized there is no mystery involved. It is not a complex, procedural process or memorization or something requiring a moving, shiny object, a blinking light or mystic chant. The alpha state is simply a state of relaxation.

At the Psychonetix Centre in Tarzana, California we make available a cassette tape recording to assist people in reaching alpha comfortably, but this is only an assist . . . to make it a bit easier. While it is convenient to relax, sit or lie down and listen to someone else take you through a verbal exercise where all you need do is listen to the voice and gentle sounds of rain, perhaps, it is something you can accomplish yourself.

All meditative practices are based upon the same principle, that of relaxation. No matter how they dress it up, whether they call it religious, philosophical or mystical, it is still the state of complete relaxation. You quiet the body and the mind by your own self-discipline.

The first step is to set aside a half-hour each day to spend solely on yourself. Be selfish about it because you deserve it. You still have twenty three and a half hours in the day to accomplish all you wish. I tell people quite frankly, if they cannot find thirty minutes out of a full day to devote to themselves it is a commentary on their own self-hatred and not life itself. It is self-hatred in the form of telling yourself you are unworthy of attending to your own well being.

Assuming you have taken the time, just sit quietly in a comfortable chair, lean back, uncross your arms and legs, close your eyes and take a few deep breaths. Beginning with your toes, engage in a one-sided conversation. Talk to your toes with your thoughts, telling them to relax. Start with the left foot . . . wiggle the toes a bit and gain awareness of their physical presence. Tell them they are now free to relax, take a rest. Talk to your body as a kind parent talks to a small child.

Send that same message of "relax" to your ankles, your calves, knees, thighs, and continue until you have encompassed the physical being from toe to scalp. Do it slowly and effortlessly, becoming aware as you do so of those parts of your body you rarely give thought. Include them and welcome them to this beautiful state of complete relaxation.

By the time you have finished with your physical being you will notice your mind has begun to drift . . . you become drowsy and dreamy. When your mind floats off in some unexpected direction, just let it go there. Should you fight it, becoming conscious of your intentions, you will activate the beta mind and the alpha state will fade and require reinforcing. Don't make your thoughts "wrong," just go with them.

In this now relaxed, drifting state, use your imagery to do something you enjoy. Go sailing or watch a sunset. If you're taking skiing lessons, see yourself gliding down a white mountainside, smiling, breathing deeply of the cool mountain air. If you enjoy bowling, do it in your mind and see yourself bowling a perfect score with the gallery cheering. Take an imaginary trip doing anything you truly enjoy.

To *use* this alpha state, simply concentrate on an outcome you desire. If it's that trip to Europe, see yourself doing it . . . walking down the Champs Elysées or cobbled streets of Scotland. Reinforce your desires by "putting it out there" into the universe. If there is someone in your life from whom you wish to hear, put that out and know they will contact you. I will not spend time here striving to convince you this will work, I will only urge you to do it . . . not with an attitude of "this is ridiculous," but with a conviction that anything is possible, so why not. Rather than effort to convince you how powerful your own attitudes and beliefs are, I will let you make this marvelous discovery for yourself.

You do have within you the ability, literally, to create the events you wish in your life. The test which will satisfy your "boss" . . . your doubting critical faculty . . . is simple. Take something you honestly feel is a bit beyond your expectations, but which you desire to come into your life. Make it something reasonable but perhaps highly improbable. It can be a new fur coat, an overseas vacation, a new relationship, whatever . . . and every day in alpha, create it actually happening. Use that powerful imagery of your own mind to make it happen. What you are doing is creating a subconscious target . . . you are aiming your mind in a specific, positive direction, the target clearly defined. Before long you will notice your "world" beginning to align to support you. "Strange coincidences" will begin to take place which your mind will attempt to discount as simple chance. What you previously thought did not exist will appear because you are now tuned in to take notice of it. You have opened a space in your own universe for it to happen.

Again, if you wish to purchase a cassette to assist you ... accelerate the rate at which you reach alpha ... you may do so, but with practice you will find it is not really necessary.

In alpha, all you are doing is planting a seed within yourself. You stop looking outside yourself for your own welfare and instead, begin creating the life you wish, internally. You quiet down, create the alpha state and then focus your creative power on a specific. Once you have it in your experience that you actually created something, even though your mind will insist it is mere coincidence, you will recognize your own tremendous power and you will never lose it.

When you go into alpha, you can use your own time clock to govern the time you spend in this regenerating, relaxing state. Your mind has its own perfect chronometer, so when you begin the process just set the time limit in your mind. I have found twenty minutes to be the time required to guarantee the alpha state. Beyond that, the state either goes higher, into beta or lower into sleep. Twenty minutes is the optimum time to practice and use alpha. So just tell yourself that in twenty minutes you will "wake up" refreshed and rested, and you will do it.

Each time you reach the alpha state you will find it becomes easier and simpler until finally, you will be relaxing almost immediately. You will become familiar with and recognize the drifting, dreamy, drowsy state. Once there, go into your imagination and create what you wish in your life.

Other than a momentary feeling of awkwardness there is nothing to keep you from using this marvelous potential of your own being. If you wish to improve your life, then simply alter your attitude about experiencing something new and different, and do it. Use your alpha regularly.

Earlier I talked about the fantastic capacity of your mental data bank . . . that reservoir for all we hold "good" and "bad," the source of our attitudes. I also said that by shoving the 12% critical faculty aside we could get into that 88% vault and transform the "bad" data or at least make ourselves aware of it. Using your imagery right now, picture your subconscious as a container with a partition down the middle. Into one side you have stored all the "bad" and into the other, the "good." If, as a small child, you were crawling along the floor and encountered a tiny mouse for the very first time, chances are you were not frightened, only curious. If you reached out and tweaked the mouse's tail, giggling as it scurried out of your reach, you looked upon the mouse as a rather funny, playful thing. It would then have been filed in the side of your memory bank marked, "good."

If, on the other hand, your mother entered the room, screamed, snatched you up in panic out of her own "bad" experiences with mice, stomped it flat . . . then it's a whole new ballgame. You are crying in fright, seeing only the bloody mess where the mouse once sat, and you are feeling, sensing your mother's own tension and horror. Now, "mouse" goes into the "bad" file and from that day forward you get to leap on chairs or run away screaming whenever you see a mouse.

When you get in touch with what is stored in this powerful memory vault, you begin to understand it through a new awareness. You can sit back and think about tiny mice with a totally new perspective and perhaps reach down and pick the mouse out of your "bad" file and put it over into the "good" file. You can even leave "mouse" right where it is but just know how it got there and how important it really is.

Your mind is yours . . . you do not belong to it. It is your faithful and obedient servant but can only do what you have programmed it to do. Get into alpha, develop your awarenesses, retain the "good" and transform or understand and come to terms with the "bad."

Everything you hold to be true *is* binding upon you. Understanding that one fact alone will start you on a lifelong journey of freedom, joy and love.

Remember we function in an abundant universe and what share of that abundance we elect to gather in for ourselves rests solely in our own attitude toward our own powers and potential. Your life is truly *how you hold it*.

Chapter 16

Alpha Breathing

Alpha Breathing is one of the most powerful and effective restorative processes available today, for a number of reasons.

1) The process itself is completely natural. It's easy, familiar, and is one that requires a minimum of instruction and can be done anywhere.

2) The process does *not* require the understanding of the Mind. As a matter of fact, the less the Mind understands, the less it can interfere with your getting results. There's nothing for the Mind to intellectualize or figure out so you won't get stuck in a lot of needless complications. All you have to do is follow the simple instructions I give you. Follow them to the letter and you will produce the desired results. I promise!

3) The process *never fails* provided you follow the instructions. Whatever happens during the exercise is what needs to happen in order for you to achieve a result.

4) Since the process is easy and based on a natural function, there are absolutely NO NEGATIVE side effects

to Alpha Breathing. You need have no fears or reservations about it being safe. The process known as "thinking" is much more hazardous to your health and well-being than is Alpha Breathing. Using the exercise daily will gradually free you from many physical, mental and emotional limitations which may have previously gone unnoticed or unrecognized. And being gradual, the changes you produce will come about in such a way as to preserve your daily way of life without confusing disturbances or upsets.

Alpha Breathing is simply a way of creating the Alpha state using the natural function of breathing; breathing which is disciplined and rhythmic. Here is how you do it.

STEP ONE: Lie down, either on the floor or on a bed. Lie flat with your head back (no pillows). If lying down is inconvenient, you can do the exercise in a recliner or a chair, but just make sure your head is tilted back. This is because you will be *breathing thru your mouth* and your jaw must be free to hang open.

STEP TWO: Close your eyes and open your mouth *wide*. Let your mouth hang open, slackened and relaxed. The wider you hang it open, the more air you can take in. Do not breathe through your nose. If you breathe through your nose you will not be doing Alpha Breathing and you will not produce the desired results.

STEP THREE: Make sure your arms and legs are uncrossed and unclasp your hands. Be sure also that your clothing is loose and nothing is binding you anywhere. It's best to remove your shoes, your glasses and your jewelry as well. Make yourself as comfortable as possible and relax.

STEP FOUR: Begin the breathing exercise. Through your mouth inhale forcefully and deliberately to lung capacity. Inhale upward as though you were drawing air up into your head. Once you reach lung capacity on the inhalation, then *immediately* exhale just as forcefully and deliberately to the point of complete exhaustion. (Don't hold your breath when your lungs are full.) Then, *immediately* inhale upward to full capacity again, then exhale deliberately again to the point of exhaustion. Inhale, exhale, inhale, exhale — deliberately, to capacity establishing a steady, unhurried rhythm *without a break or interruption* between the inhale and the exhale. Breathe audibly so you can hear yourself as you create this "connnected" breathing. Breathe in this manner for twenty minutes without stopping.

At the end of twenty minutes, let go of the exercise completely and just drift off into a natural state of reverie that the Alpha Breathing produces. You might mistake this state of reverie for falling asleep but never mind. It is during this reverie that the process restores, refreshes, and rehabilitates you on all three levels — physical, emotional, and mental. During this time notice what pictures your mind brings up, if any. By pictures I mean memories, images, or fantasies. Since the exercise is non-intellectual, you needn't concern yourself with "positive thoughts" or suggestions. You don't have to fret about what to say to yourself. You don't even have to create pictures or imagine anything. Just kick back and notice what happens during the exercise.

Here are a few things you may notice during the Alpha Breathing.

1) For the first few times (there is no set number) you will notice that your hands and feet become very cold. Cold is a sign of accumulated tension stored in the extremeties. As you do the connected breathing, this tension surfaces almost immediately. KEEP BREATHTING because the breathing is what releases it. Once you've released this old

tension from your body, you will be delighted to notice that your hands and feet will stay toasty warm from then on, regardless of the weather or temperature. In short while each time you do the exercise, your hands and feet will literally glow with warmth and energy and soon that energy will gradually spread thru your limbs and into your whole body (this is great for muscle aches, tension and stiffness). Watch your body respond with this new vitality and energy!

2) For a while (again, no set number of times) your hands will seem to take on a life of their own. While you are doing the breathing exercise, your fingers will stiffen and get all "funny" (stored toxins and tension). Then, your hands will begin to move quite on their own — upwards usually toward your face. Don't worry about this as it is quite natural. Once the coldness subsides, this movement will become less and less and eventually stop altogether. And those "funny" stiff fingers will loosen and soften and gradually begin to glow.

3) You'll begin the breathing exercise with your mouth wide open but as you progress your mouth may begin to pucker up as though you were about to whistle. Just keep breathing and again, this will pass as you release old tension.

4) Connected breathing initially produces noticeable dizziness. Again, don't worry about this. You are already lying down so you won't fall anywhere. The dizziness occurs simply because you are getting much more oxygen into your brain cells (hoorah!!) and these cells are being energized and activated. This activation initially manifests as dizziness but eventually stops altogether and you then manifest better memory, more mental vitality and even a higher IQ!! You are also getting more oxygen into your body cells which results in more energy, physical vitality and strength.

People are, by training and agreement, ordinarily lousy

breathers. Their breathing is ragged, shallow, hardly noticeable and lacking in force, sound, and vigor. Is it any wonder that sickness and pain is our nation's number one industry. Breathing is our umbilical to life and that connection must be maintained vigorously!

Hyperventilation is a term the medical industry has applied to vigorous breathing to discourage each of us from taking deep, connected breaths of air. Pity! We are even encouraged to put a sack over our heads in order to inhale back into our systems our own carbon dioxide in order to short cut this "ailment" of hyperventilation. In reality the ailment is subventilation. That is, shallow, inhibited breathing which is what is called "normal." People who breath vigorously find it impossible to hyperventilate. They are active, vital, healthy people who are *very connected* to life and reality. They enjoy life fully since their *connectedness* produces a much lower level of fear. They have literally, "breathed their fears away."

Now, once again, lie down, stretch out and make yourself comfortable. Open your mouth wide, close your eyes and inhale, exhale, inhale, exhale deeply, fully to capacity/exhaustion for twenty minutes without stopping. (You can use an ordinary kitchen timer to preset your time limit.) During the twenty minutes you will notice the coldness in your hands and feet as well as the "funny" fingers and hand movements. As you breathe slowly, steadily, deliberately, rhythmically, *connectedly*, you will also notice some dizziness. KEEP BREATHING! Whatever you notice happening, KEEP BREATHING! This is a most important point. *Do not stop until your time is up.* Your mind will do everything it can to discourage you from going on with this.

Once your twenty minutes are over, just let go and drift

off into that nice, dreamy state of reverie (Alpha). You will snooze for another ten or fifteen minutes. Then, you're done for that session. Get up and go about your business. It's just that simple. You'll feel refreshed, invigorated and in high spirits.

How frequently you do the Alpha Breathing exercise is strictly up to you. Doing this daily produces the best results. Two or three times a week takes longer and produces a lower level of response. (You won't really start to glow, you'll just tingle a lot.) Doing the exercise once in a while will only serve to discourage you completely. This exercise serves not only to create the Alpha state but it also retrains your breathing as it expands your ability to deal with every aspect of daily living.

What's Alpha Breathing use for? Many things — its uses are as varied as the people who learn to do it. Here are just a few areas where Alpha breathing is highly effective:

1) *Depression* — You simply cannot maintain an ongoing depressive state and do the Alpha Breathing exercise. You cannot mix fire and water; you cannot stay depressed and breathe deep. For anyone who suffers depression, six weeks of daily Alpha Breathing can make all the difference in the world. No drugs or pills, no talk-talk, no hassles, just breathing. And that does it!

2) *Grief (suffering a loss)* — This exercise has proven to be nothing short of miraculous for those who have suffered a loss and are grieving. Grief vanishes after only a short four week daily program of Alpha Breathing.

3) *Upsets* — Upsets have nothing to do with what's going on with you at the moment. Upsets are old, unresolved feelings that are unconsciously triggered by something in the present and these old feelings crop up. So, during an upset (fear, anger, anxiety, worry, frustration,

etc.) remember to BREATHE! Then, the first chance you get afterward, do the full twenty minute exercise. In time your upsets will subside completely (yes indeed) and they will disappear for good. You won't even know why but so what. You must do the full exercise regularly.

4) *Insomnia* — Insomnia also vanishes in a couple of weeks of daily sleep breathing. Nothing else works faster or more easily than this. Just breathe and sleep.

5) *Tension and Stress* — As an ongoing condition, stress/tension produces high blood pressure, hypertension, heart trouble, stomach ailments and a whole host of disorders. Daily deep breathing will gradually restore you completely as it reduces the strain on all your vital organs. Thus relieved, you will experience physically progressive greater harmony and balance in your day to day living. The effects are accumulative.

6) *Athletics* — Daily deep breathing creates incredible stamina and vitality. The lungs are crucial to athletics which explains the emphasis on jogging. Really, it isn't the exercise of jogging that makes the difference, it's the expanded breathing.

There are so many uses for Alpha Breathing that I could go on for pages relating change after change people have achieved doing this deep breathing regularly. If you choose to do this exercise, and if you'd like to share your achievements with others then simply write to us and let us know what you've done and what your experience was. Our address is in the front of this book. We look forward to hearing from you.

Thus we have a simple, easy, natural process by which we can all restore and rehabilitate our skill to deal with the rigors and stresses of daily living, and come out the better for it. Alpha Breathing will be very shortly recognized, I'm sure, for the effective, marvelous tool that it is. Enjoy it. Use it daily. Use it and stay well!

SELF-IMPROVEMENT

Let's take a look at the priorities on which people spend their money. What comes first? The rent: and this is the worst investment on the list. Compare rent with self-improvement. You paid $6.00 for this book and you get to use this information forever. The fact is that self-improvement is the most valuable item of your budget and most people don't even have a category for it.

Fear of running out causes you to spend only on things people told you to spend money on. When it comes to buying things that are really good for you and that make you happy, guilt comes. When you say, "I don't have enough money to go to that self-improvement seminar, or buy that self-improvement book," it is almost like saying, "I am not a good investment."

The best way to make money is to invest it in yourself, and that is what self-improvement is all about.

So take a look at re-doing your budget and making self-improvement the top priority. It works!